the BEST SEVEN YEARS *of my life*

THE STORY OF AN UNLIKELY CAREGIVER

GEORGE SHANNON
CHAD PATRICK SHANNON

First Printing: 2018

ISBN: 978-1-7326455-3-0

To Ma Mère and Pops,
for not only living with true grit and great spirit,
but for their courage in sharing their lives for this book.

CONTENTS

foreword   1

CHAPTER ONE
the moment of change   5

CHAPTER TWO
dedication   21

CHAPTER THREE
unrelenting   33

CHAPTER FOUR
a search for inner peace   45

CHAPTER FIVE
the healing power of humility   55

CHAPTER SIX
better days   63

CHAPTER SEVEN
whether tragedy or turkey   81

CHAPTER EIGHT
feel the love   91

CHAPTER NINE
it finds you   105

CONTENTS

CHAPTER TEN
the mighty fight   115

CHAPTER ELEVEN
on her own two feet   129

CHAPTER TWELVE
for the rest of my years   137

foreword

Steve Thomas
Sewickley, Pa

"… for better, for worse, for richer, for poorer, in sickness and in health, 'til death do us part" is a traditional Christian marriage vow derived from the Book of Common Prayer in 17th Century England (when the average lifespan was about thirty-five years). Given today's longevity, a lifetime commitment whatever life brings can truly be a heavy one. The Best Seven Years of My Life is a love story that describes how George Shannon honors those vows as tragedy strikes when his wife Carol suffers strokes, and when it first becomes clear that she is going to need someone to care for her every hour of every day.

Most people's reaction to these circumstances would be to tumble into depression. Life has dealt you a bad hand. You're boxed in. It would have been so much easier for George to find someone else to take care of her than to do it himself. Bring strangers into the house to offer round-the-clock care. Put Carol in a home. Take the easy way out. But that isn't George. Self-pity wasn't an option for him. If he ever felt sorry for himself, he never showed it. He was all in.

When the relationship faced its drastic change, George totally accepted his fate and grew from it. He recognized anew that he was, as he puts it, "terribly in love with this woman." He found joy in a seemingly never-ending task that would buckle most of us at the knees. He moved into a state of "agape love," a Greco-Christian term describing the highest form of love known to humanity—a transcendent, unconditional, selfless love that commits one passionately to the wellbeing of others and persists regardless of circumstance. It is love with no expectation of reciprocity.

George talks about his relationship with Carol in delightfully amusing ways. After the strokes, her personality changed. She lost the filter that kept her from blurting out personal thoughts that might be considered inappropriate for public consumption. This resulted in Carol developing a sudden, unexpected, and riotously funny sense of humor. It changed their relationship in ways that brought George great joy, even as so much about his daily life also had to change.

George's depth of caring for Carol is truly spiritually uplifting, but the greatest surprise of all is how his expression of selfless love changed him. I relate this from the position of an insider, a close friend of George and his family for thirty years. Like many male friendships, ours was initially based upon similar interests—golf trips, poker, and jovial camaraderie over too many cocktails. Our competitive natures drew us to each other, fueled by testosterone, ego, and a mutual enjoyment of challenging one another, both verbally and in games of skill. George was a man's man, a pot-stirrer, someone you would undoubtedly enjoy having a drink with. However, a dramatic shift in his temperament was in store. As George devoted himself to Carol's wellbeing, he became a humbler, more compassionate and spiritual human being. He opened himself to vulnerability, noting that "self-defense is really not important anymore."

The Best Seven Years of My Life provides a template for others facing similar circumstances as they seek comfort and inspiration to rise above their travails. I only hope they have the good fortune to read this book and take from it the knowledge that love (and love alone) can carry us through times that can truly seem too much to bear. There is nothing wrong—and in fact, there is a lot right—with accepting and showing the softer side of your soul. When you do this, you don't have to decide how you will deal with a caregiver situation; you will find ways to accept it, embrace it, and figure out how to make your life not just as good as it ever was, but better.

CHAPTER ONE
the moment of change

We can love completely without complete understanding.
– Norman Maclean
A River Runs Through It and Other Stories

January 2017

My eyes opened to the digital numbers projected on the bedroom ceiling: 4:02 A.M., large and red. The recent years had shaped in me a powerful fixation on time. How many minutes had passed since the last time Carol woke me? Would it be better to administer her insulin five minutes or twenty minutes before breakfast? When exactly were the doctor appointments today, and what time was her physical therapy session at the rehab facility?

How long would Carol live? How long would I live?

By the time I'd shaken off enough sleep to sit up, my wife had already managed to get her little legs out of the bed. She didn't have the strength to climb down on her own, and even in the heavy darkness, I could see her big, white, fuzzy socks dangling high above the floor. There was no telling how many times she'd gotten herself stuck in this position while trying to wake me. My hearing had been going, and even before the stroke, Carol's voice was often hushed.

"I see you've got those Tweety legs ready to go," I said, my voice groggy as I delivered the same joke I'd been telling for more than forty-seven years of marriage.

"They are what they are," Carol deadpanned.

I forced my fatigued body to shuffle over to her side of the bed. Her walker awaited me, but since it would only slow us down anyway, I decided to help her to the bathroom without it. I sat her straight up and wrapped my arms around her. She was a tiny thing. For as long as I'd known her, she'd claimed to be over five feet tall, but a trip to the doctor's office just yesterday had finally confirmed the sheer egregiousness of that fib. The truth was closer to four feet, ten inches.

Photo: Carol with her favorite teddy bear.

5

Balance was often a fickle friend to Carol, so I made sure to secure her arms tightly before bringing her to her feet. "I have to go really bad," she reported, drawing out the urgency of the really.

"Gotcha, honey," I replied.

We held tight to each other as we waddled to the bathroom. Since the strokes, Carol's gait had been much more of a short-stepped shuffle than a walk. Just like her physical therapists, I would often encourage her to take larger steps. Halfway through the journey, I grabbed her hand and took a step too fast for her.

"You have the wrong arm," she said.

She'd broken her right shoulder a few years back, and it still pained her to put weight on it. I slowed up to release the pressure. It probably came from a place of cranky exhaustion, but I remember thinking that it would've been nice if she'd included a "please."

When we arrived at our destination, Carol reached for the silver grab-bar we'd had installed, then let gravity do the rest as she plopped down on the seat.

"Another safe landing," she announced.

I chuckled as I lumbered out of the room to give her some modicum of privacy. The poor woman probably couldn't remember the last time she'd been left totally alone. I couldn't have been more than a step past the white-framed doorway before she called out to me.

"I think I'm done."

"Let's maybe wait another minute before we go back to bed," I suggested, my tone a mixed bag of hope and directive.

She quickly agreed, so I returned to the edge of the bed and did some plopping down of my own.

Getting up frequently wasn't anything new, but this night had been particularly rough. We'd had to wake seven times since we first went to bed during the eleven o'clock news. On the sixth time, just an hour before this latest occasion, Carol had failed to wake before trouble struck. Early in this phase of our relationship, an accident in the bed might have frustrated me, but by now, I'd performed the routine so many times I'd lost count. It had become almost mechanical. Immediately, I would go into the preprogrammed twenty-five-minute cleanup mode: Get Carol out of bed, change her clothes, help her wash herself, strip the sheets, start a load of laundry, make the bed again, and get her back to sleep.

From opposite sides of the room, we sat in silence for a moment before I heard Carol's signature rustling. For years, whenever she found herself near anything made of disposable paper—usually napkins, tissues, or toilet paper—she would fidget with it. She would fold it up and rub it on her lips, back and forth, producing that slight rustling sound. A few doctors had told me that this was likely a symptom of Vascular Parkinsonism, but we couldn't be sure.

The sound from the bathroom stopped for a second, drawing my attention. Carol had honored my request for an additional minute almost to the second, but now she was ready for help. So I began the slow, lumbering process of returning her to bed.

I sat her back into bed the same way I'd helped her up. Before she lay down, I reached over and adjusted her necklace, a silver caged heart I'd purchased in a bumbled romantic gesture on Valentine's Day many years ago. Carol wore this necklace every day, but through the night, the pendant and the chain's clasp would get bunched up on the back of her neck, so whenever I could, I would bring the pendant back to the front.

"Thank you," she said in the kindest of voices, as she always did.

As I tucked her in, I couldn't wait to lie down and maybe get the most of the next forty-five minutes—when, like clockwork, I could expect to be roused from sleep again. I hit the lights, crumbled back into bed, and covered myself. Fifteen seconds passed before the covers started to rustle again, and I knew what was coming next.

"I don't think I finished," Carol said, a tinge of apology in her voice.

I should have known better than to get comfortable. Powered by a deep sigh, I found the energy to chuck the covers aside and start the routine once more. I delivered her to the bathroom, then returned to my usual waiting spot on the bed, where I stared straight into the darkness and wondered how many times we had gotten up in the middle of the night to do this. It had been almost seven years since the event that changed our lives. Eighty months. *Multiply the months by thirty,* I thought, doing the math. *So, roughly 2,400 nights, at an average of five times per night.*

"Twelve thousand times," I whispered.

It was late April of 2010, right around my birthday. My sister Barbara had earned a free trip to Cabo for her fine sales work at Howard

7

Hannah Real Estate the previous year. Carol and I would be meeting her, along with my brothers Jimmy and Tommy and everyone's spouses, for a few days of rest and relaxation. It had been a busy spring at my job as the vice president of sales for the northern district of a water tank maintenance company, so a free trip that promised beaches, family, cocktails, and nothing to do but relax sounded like just about all I could ever ask for.

Our plane began its descent. A long way down the peninsula, on the Pacific side of Mexico, awaited Cabo San Lucas. The plane skirted the water line as we neared the little airport. Beneath us stretched a ribbon of idyllic beach, and even from 5,000 feet up, I could practically feel the fine, light-brown sand between my toes. The sky was a shade of blue whose match I'd never seen before, even in my forty years in the paint business.

As we exited the airport, we were met by a perfect breeze and comfortable evening weather. The fading sun felt warm on my skin.

Carol and I passed our twenty-minute taxi ride from the airport in the same way we'd passed the flight, and frankly, the same way we'd passed most of our time of late: in total silence, like we were leading two separate lives. I would work with my salesmen all day while Carol ran her daily errands like clockwork. At the end of the day, I would go to the driving range to work on my golf swing while Carol would plow through one book after another. We would meet up around dinner time, the meal or restaurant often left to my choice. On the weekends, I would golf with my friends while she talked on the phone with hers and read her books. She rarely tried to initiate much in our lives. Everything we did was on me to plan and schedule, including any social activity.

The more I pondered, the more I realized that Carol and I had slipped into an extended stale phase. We had been married for forty-one years, and our three kids were all grown now. In their youth, they had led active sporting lives, their athletic endeavors keeping our social calendars full, but those days had become faded memories. Our oldest son, Sean, worked in the financial world in New York City. Our youngest, Matthew, made his home and work in Montana. Chad, the middle son, lived in Pittsburgh but was often busy with his legal career and social life. Carol and I had expected to be grandparents by then, but none of the kids were married.

In this way, ours had become a boring existence. This didn't mean we didn't love each other, just that we'd grown weary. And tension was a little high between us at this moment, because somewhere over Arizona, I'd made the mistake of finally asking her if we could get rid of some of the *Vanity Fair, People,* and other assorted magazines piling up in our house. In her defense, my tone could've been politer, but at the same time, I'd just never understood why she couldn't bring herself to throw those old issues away. More than anything, though, I'd just wanted her to take a strong position on the matter, one way or another. But as was Carol's tendency, she'd shrugged off my request and retreated into silence. I had always read this as an unwillingness on her part to be a full partner in our marriage. This made me feel alone.

Instead of asking about the magazines, I turned my frustration inward. *Why are you getting hung up on this small stuff?* I thought. I figured maybe I should try cheering myself up by reading the little black notebook I'd filled with positive or insightful quotes to remember. I'd been leaning on that book more often than usual lately, as the effort to build a new sales territory from scratch was often stressful, and reading those sayings always soothed my anxiety. Whenever I needed a breath, I would find one of my dad's quotes like "Make it a great day today," or if I had gotten too uptight about work, I would look for that truism, "Nobody on his deathbed ever said I wished I'd spent more time in the office."

At the resort, Barbara, her wide grin a fond reminder of our father, greeted us at the door of a spacious four-bedroom unit held together by a large communal area. Her infectious joy at having the whole family together managed to chase away what remained of my annoyance about the silence and the magazines, but even through the next few days of fun, laughter, and goofy jokes, I just couldn't seem to relax.

Whenever Carol and I had a few free moments together, we didn't talk much, and the chilly indifference hanging between us only heightened my sense of restlessness.

On our last full day of the trip, it finally occurred to me that the best way to make amends would be to try to squeeze out some time for Carol and me to spend alone. Eventually, I worked up the nerve to ask the question that had been churning in my mind all morning. "Why don't we do our own thing for lunch today?"

She reacted as if she hadn't heard me.

I approached and stood by her side. "Did you hear me?" I asked, immediately regretting the frustration I heard in my own voice.

"I think I'd rather just do lunch as a group today," Carol said with the level of calm that meant she was trying to avoid conflict.

Even though I knew I shouldn't allow myself to storm out of the bedroom, that's exactly what I did. Frankly, I wanted her to tell me that I was a jerk, or explain why she was upset with me. I never had any idea what she was thinking, and that lack of connection was painful. But instead of turning around and addressing those thoughts with her, I went for a walk. When I came back twenty minutes later, she'd gone with the others to the village of Cabo.

And every day since, I've pondered the question at least once: What would I be willing to trade if it meant that I could go back and change that moment? The answer, with confidence, is *anything*. I would give anything to be able to warn my sulking sack of a younger self about how drastically our lives were about to change. I didn't know it during that sun-soaked morning, but this would be the last solo conversation I would ever have with the Carol I used to know.

After a relaxing day and an early dinner, the group returned to the suite with the intention of grabbing a nightcap. I enjoyed an orange vodka as I settled into the charade of trying to read with a distracted mind.

"Hey, Georgie," Jimmy said from across the room. He was shuffling a deck of cards. "I've got a seat at the poker table for you over here. Fifty cents a hand. I know you like a high-stakes game."

"Come on, George, sit next to your big sister," Barbara chimed in.

"I'm getting into this book," I lied. "Maybe in a little while."

"Suit yourself, buddy," Jimmy said, totally oblivious to the tremendous effort I was putting in to make a show of pouting. "I plan on making a killing over here."

This started Barbara on one of her stories, "Oh God, Jim, do you remember that one time we were at the track with Mom?"

"Before you get into that story about horses," Tommy said, "you'd better pony up the ante."

Tommy's puns always had a way of causing Barbara to go into hysterics. "You'd better rein it in before this party gets crazy," she said once she'd caught her breath.

Carol was smiling that cute little smile everyone loved. It was that same smile that had so often coaxed my dad to share his stories, Carol's nieces to divulge their latest boyfriend updates at the kitchen table, or one of our sons to disclose his challenges at school or work.

The smile convinced me, like it had so many times in the past, that the time had finally come to quit pouting. All I needed was an opening to work my way into the game.

"I'm getting a beer," Jimmy announced, right on cue. "Play this one without me."

This was my chance. But before I could get up, my brother was already at my side.

"Take a good look at Carol," Jimmy said in a voice just above a whisper. "She's playing one-handed."

I stood back and watched for a while, and sure enough, Carol would pick up her cards with her right hand, then set them down and use the same hand to flip them whenever her turn came. My wife had always been rather unorthodox in the fine-motor department, so I figured maybe it was just a fluke. But then, over the next couple hands, it became clear that she was going out of her way to avoid using her left. Lately, Carol had been subject to occasional bouts with mini-strokes, episodes that left her dazed or otherwise acting a bit strange. Frightening as they were, there was really nothing we could do about them except visit the doctor as soon as possible. As I watched her playing with only her right hand, I knew it would be better to ask the resort to send in a local doctor rather than waiting until tomorrow's return to the States.

An hour later, the doctor arrived, and Carol told him about her type II diabetes and the mini-strokes. He looked her over, checked her vitals, and since her hand seemed to have improved, advised that she was likely either dehydrated or suffering from low blood sugar. She drank some orange juice and perked up quickly.

Once the excitement had died down, I finally worked my way into the card game. I listened to Tommy's jokes, watched Barbara bask in the glory of her family, tried not to let Jim win all the money, and indulged in my relief that my wife seemed okay.

Around four o'clock in the morning, I woke from an unstill sleep to find that Carol wasn't in bed. I figured she'd just gotten up to use the bathroom, but after a few minutes passed, worry crept into my mind, and I rose to go look for her.

In the bathroom, the image of Carol that greeted me was one I'll never be able to chase from my memory. She was sitting on the floor with her legs folded, Indian-style, as she stared at the ceiling. Not a day goes by that I don't wonder what was happening in her mind.

"Carol!" I cried out as I rushed to her. "What's going on?"

She just looked at me and smiled.

"Honey, what happened?"

My wife of over forty years didn't seem to recognize me. She gazed right through me for a moment, and then, trapped in some mental space I couldn't reach, she returned her attention to the ceiling, the grin frozen on her face. A moment of tremendous terror seized me from head to toe before I snapped back to reality. I could fret myself sick later, but for now, Carol needed medical attention.

My first instinct was to take her to the local hospital, but I knew nothing about the quality of the Mexican healthcare system, so I quickly started running through scenarios that would get Carol back to the States as soon as possible. I'd flown enough in my life to know that no airline would board a passenger in this condition. Fortunately, one of my oldest friends in the world was Rich Ryan, a pilot who had spent his career running various private jet companies. The expense would be overwhelming, but I dialed Rich's number and asked him for an enormous favor.

Rich was just working out the details on how he could dispatch a plane from California to Cabo when Carol started to vomit. Each time she got sick, my heart raced a little faster, and I questioned a little harder whether I should abandon the flight idea and just find the nearest emergency room. I was right on the verge of changing course when it started to seem like the worst had passed. She still had that vacant look in her eyes, but it had been a long time since she'd vomited, and a bit of color had returned to her face. So we drove to the airport and boarded Rich's eight-seater plane.

The seats were set up to face each other, four to a side. I sat across from Carol so I could keep an eye on her. At the moment of takeoff, I realized that I'd never been so terrified. We were set to fly over an incredibly barren stretch of land, and it seemed to me that if Carol's condition deteriorated, her chances of survival ranged from slim to none. Each moment that passed carried a simultaneous charge of relief that she was still fighting, and dread that the next instant might short-circuit her brain forever. If that happened, then I would have to live with the knowledge that our last solo conversation had been more like a fight.

For the next four hours, I stared into my wife's eyes, looking for changes and searching for clues to her wellbeing. Each time I asked her whether she was okay, she would reply with a wide-eyed, perpetual grin like I'd just told her the best joke of all time. My desperation to know what was happening in her mind was almost more than I could bear. I'd always been a fixer of things, but this time, my toolbox lay empty. I'd never felt so helpless.

The longer I took in Carol's expression, the more I recognized something in those eyes that I had too long taken for granted. It was trust. She had always trusted in me no matter what decision I'd made: where we lived, my career path, how many children to have. She'd put her wholesale faith in me in a way that made me realize how much she counted on me.

Then, sometime after changing planes in San Diego, and somewhere over the southwestern United States, with Carol's eyes still locked on mine, I came to a truth that forever altered the direction of my life. I told myself that if Carol survived this, then I would devote my life to making hers better. I would do whatever it took to make her healthy again. With that vow, an all-consuming feeling transcended the anxiety which had racked my world all day long:

I'm terribly in love with this woman.

For one glorious moment, that emotion filled my whole body. As the plane landed in Pittsburgh and we taxied toward the gate, I could see my son Chad's silver Hyundai Sonata awaiting us on the tarmac. Together, we carried Carol off the plane and into Chad's car. When we arrived, the doctors and nurses took Carol straight back.

The waiting room at Allegheny General's ER—a room with which I would become all too familiar—was a large, white-walled, brightly lit area lined with perpetually glowing televisions. There was as much stale coffee as your heart desired. And the tables here and there were piled high with magazines that I never got around to reading. Carol would've loved that.

We'd been up since four in the morning, had traveled thirteen hours on planes, and had been focused the whole time on getting home. With Carol in able hands, my mind could finally start organizing the questions. Our uncertain future weighed the heaviest.

"What am I going to do?" I asked Chad several times.

Neither of us had an answer.

This led me to a deluge of further questions: how long before Carol would recover and be her old self again? In the meantime, how would I manage her care? And was I even capable of doing it on my own?

Then, the darker questions: what if she didn't recover? What if this was how it would always be? And then, the darkest questions: what if I would never be able to apologize to her for our last conversation? What if I would never get another chance to tell her how much I loved her? What if my wife died?

All night, I battled with these unanswerable questions. People came and went, shifts changed, and as the sun rose the next morning, Carol was finally admitted to the Stroke Unit on the ninth floor. This brought some small measure of relief, as I'd admired the staff from that unit ever since Carol was a patient there for her mini-strokes in February of 2009.

Her room was right next to the nurses' station, which added to my growing sense of comfort. Soon, I spotted the familiar face of Dr. Ashis Tayal in the hallway as he conversed with his team. Up to that point, I had never met a doctor who balanced bedside manner with the ability to be frank with such perfection. We were in good hands. I just knew that if anyone could make Carol better, it was Dr. Tayal.

The official diagnosis was as good as Greek to me: a right anterior cerebral infarct. Ultimately, the stroke had affected the area of Carol's brain responsible for the movement of her legs, her left arm, and the initiation of speech. Her decision-making would also be impacted. The diagnosis of expressive aphasia meant that there could be some speaking and writing issues as well, but the doctor was confident that this condition could be improved. Overall, the news was as good as could be expected.

Carol was released only six days later and sent to a local rehabilitation facility for physical, occupational, and speech therapy. As a lifelong devotee of planning—and as the kind of person who writes lists for everything from shopping to the next day's chores, and even books I wanted to someday read—I reveled in the thoroughness of the plan the doctors had set up for us. We now had a clear path to Carol's return to full health, and I knew that as long as we followed that path step by step, all would be well.

Of course, it all depended on how Carol would take to rehab. Much to my surprise, she seemed more determined than ever, eating everything they put in front of her, completing every exercise they prescribed her, and even asking to be walked down the hall for additional exercise. Carol had hated exercise for as long as I could remember. Often, when I drove home from work, I would find her car parked in our friend Maris Moriarty's driveway precisely one block away from our house, and I would shake my head every time. She couldn't walk one block to visit her friend?

But now here she was, digging into her rehab, and all that hard work soon paid off. On May 22, 2010, exactly one month since I had found her in a daze on the floor of a bathroom in Cabo San Lucas, my wife was discharged home.

Hand in hand, we stepped through the front door of our two-story house in the little borough of Edgeworth, Pennsylvania, and those questions that had hounded me in the emergency room seemed so far away. Carol hadn't completely recovered from the stroke, but full recovery was in sight. All we had to do was take her regularly to outpatient therapy, so she could improve on her mobility and vocal expression.

The moment we got through our front door, a clock on the wall reminded me that Carol needed to take her medicine. So I sat her down and searched our bags and the car. I could only find prescriptions. She'd been on an extensive list of medications at the facility, but the staff had failed to send me home with any for immediate use or advise me to pick up new ones. I had no idea what to do or how to get Carol's pills, and I knew that the clock was ticking.

Thankfully, a local nurse, Sandy Travato, had heard Carol was being discharged and came to check in on us. A savior of sorts, Sandy arrived out of nowhere, took one look at Carol, and sent us to the local emergency room. They discovered that her blood sugar had spiked to 400 and gave her an insulin shot.

Meanwhile, Sandy had dropped off and picked up a full set of prescriptions from our local pharmacy, and we had everything back in order by nightfall.

After dinner, we finished our hectic day by sitting together on the couch for the first time in a month. All three of our sons called in to congratulate their mother on making it home, a fact that made me smile, because there was a time when my wife worried that her children would never love her like they did me. I still think about that anxiety often. It all came to a head one late summer day. I'd been tossing the baseball with Chad and Matthew when Sean came running through the kitchen and out the back door to tell me about his football practice and how they were going to make him a running back. It was a happy moment, but when I returned into the house, I found Carol crying at the kitchen table.

"What's wrong?" I asked, rushing to her.

It took her a moment to collect herself enough to speak. "I just don't understand why the boys never want to spend time with me," she said, gazing up at me with those dewy eyes of hers that made her look like she was always on the edge of laughter, even when sad.

"What do you mean?"

"I'll never be able to connect with them with sports like you do."

"You connect with them in other ways."

She dismissed the thought with a turn of her head. "Sean was so excited to tell you about football. But he didn't bother telling me."

My heart skipped a beat. I didn't know what to say, so instead of offering immediate hope, I looked to the future. "When our boys become men," I said, "everything will be different. You'll see."

Now here we sat in our living room, having just finished the last of the three calls from our sons, and I could see that I had been right all those years ago. The boys adored their mother and had every intention of becoming a more consistent presence in our lives.

Carol passed the next hour watching one of her favorite talent show contests on TV, and I, as I'm prone to do, fell into a deep state of thinking about the drastic changes since that moment in Mexico. Even before our vacation, and perhaps fueled by having recently elected to receive my first social security retirement check, I'd been pondering the reason for my life. On paper I'd accomplished so much, but beyond raising my three sons, I felt like I was missing true fulfillment.

My wife's stroke had presented the worthy purpose of nursing her back to health. In the first month, I'd been there every step of the way, and those efforts made me feel good. Yet the minor fiasco with the pills and insulin had shown that I could do better. I could learn more about her condition, seek out healthier meals to make for us, and research new therapies. Most importantly, I needed to be a more complete husband.

The moment I devoted myself to Carol on the plane had been tender, but it also opened my eyes. It made me realize that I had somehow allowed inflexibility to take hold in our daily lives. A sneaky thing that way, the power of stubbornness had deposited its energy into cleanliness, routine, and order: my yard had to be landscaped a certain way, my house had to be clean, my personal things organized to my liking, and even my meals had to contain certain foods. Over time, I had hoarded the focus of our marriage and didn't even recognize how selfish I had become.

Whenever my expectations weren't met, I would succumb to prolonged periods of dwelling, and of festering to the point of general gloominess, which led me to, as my mother used to say, being "testy." The cranky person on the vacation in Cabo San Lucas came from this place. My crabbiness over the magazines ran much deeper than a cluttered home.

In this way, I also realized that Carol would need more than just my commitment. I would have to dig deep to recapture a facet of myself that I had let decay for much too long: a sense of humility. Some twenty years before, I had come to an understanding of the beauty of humility and the proper tools to maintain it, but those insights had faded with time. Over those years, my mind had been filled with the gunk of pride.

Though I'd turned my full attention to Carol over the past month, irritable George intruded on my dedication to her and invaded my mind with self-centered questions about whether I'd end up resenting my wife if she didn't get better, or got worse someday. To triumph, I'd need to confront my demons and rediscover the path to humility. In our uncertain future, would that darker side of my personality come through, or would I would find a better part of me?

A vague sense of unease crept in as I wondered whether I would succeed in achieving that purpose of returning Carol to health. More harrowing was the notion that I had no idea how much longer we would have together—she might live another ten years, even another twenty, or another stroke could take her away from us in the next moment.

I reached out for her hand under the blanket and gave it a good squeeze. She turned to me and let a little smile form on her face. In that smile, all the answers became clear: deep down, even though I had always struggled to love myself, I loved Carol with all my heart. For however long we had together, I would try my best to make sure she always knew it.

The bedroom was still dark. I peeked at the trusty red numbers on the ceiling: 4:13 A.M. Outside, the birds had already begun their predawn chirping.

"Can you come get me?" Carol asked from her perch in the bathroom.

I found her standing and holding onto the grab-bar. She blinked and smiled at me, anxious for my return. Any agitation I might have felt about the early hour or the lack of sleep or the damn birds stood no chance against this love.

Together, we started our slow amble to the mirror. No matter what the time was, Carol had to fix her hair before leaving any bathroom. After a few quick passes at her bangs, she set the brush down. Then, her hand holding mine tight, she nuzzled into my shoulder.

"Thank you for all you do for me," she said.

Back in bed, I pulled the covers over her. Then, I handed her the little brown teddy bear our youngest son Matthew had given her after her first major stroke seven years ago. She held it close. She never went to bed without it.

As I slid closer to her, I found her free hand, held it up to her cheek, squeezed tight, and did the last thing I always did before we returned to sleep.

"I love my Carol," I sang to her, terribly off-key.

"I love my Pogey," she replied with a giggle.

Within minutes, I heard her little snore. I stared at those big digital numbers on that cold January night: 4:18 A.M. In a few minutes, I would doze off, and about thirty minutes later, she would likely get me up again. In those moments before my little bouts of sleep, I thanked God for the little human embodiment of perseverance and positivity sleeping next to me. She was a wee-sized woman who defined a toughness and grit I had never known existed, someone who never let her relentless health problems get her down. What I couldn't have known back then, and what I never would have been able to face, was that my Carol would be gone less than three months later.

As I look back now, I know one thing for sure: Despite the day to day challenge between those two Aprils in 2010 and 2017, those were the best seven years of my life. This is my recollection of my time taking care of Carol. It's a tale of an unlikely caregiver, a journey toward rediscovering humility, and the story of a man blessed with the amazing chance to fall in love all over again.

I cannot control what happens to me.
I can, however, control how I react to it.

– Epictetus

CHAPTER TWO
dedication

June 1, 2010

From day one after Carol's discharge from the rehab center, I had begun making good on my promise to help her get back to her original self. We weren't going to merely accept the changes in our life; we were going to attack them. We followed an aggressive strategy for her care and therapy and kept to a regimented schedule. Until I could get the house ready for her to live in with some semblance of independence, she would spend her days in a safe place with people facing similar situations. It pained me to have to leave her in a local adult daycare center, but I knew that the process of repurposing our home to accommodate her care would require a great deal of my time and focus. So during the day, at least, it felt like it made more sense to set her up in a place where she could receive the extra attention she needed.

The first task in the effort to rebuild our lives would be the simplest: dispose of our poor eating habits. After dropping Carol off for her first day at the center, I drove to a nearby organic market to buy healthy food to replace all the junk I had cleaned out of the cupboards the night before. For two hours, I walked the aisles and studied the unfamiliar labels of a wide variety of health foods like Ezekiel bread and wild-caught salmon filets. The effort filled me with a joyful sense that we were both going to change our lives for the better, would meet the many challenges ahead of us, and we would keep to this new routine until normalcy returned.

Around lunchtime, I returned to the daycare facility to check on Carol. I found her throwing up, sick as a dog. I didn't bother waiting for an ambulance. By the time we hit the highway, I noticed that her eyes had assumed a distant, almost lost sort of glaze—a look that said she could go at any moment. We'd been told that a second stroke could happen, but neither of us could have imagined that it would crash down on her quite so soon. A consuming dread gripped my chest as I sped

---

Photo: George's favorite picture of Carol, at the house on Thorn Street.

down the four-lane highway. I felt helpless, like we were plodding through wet cement toward a brighter future that would never come.

Full speed ahead, I flew toward Pittsburgh in whatever lane of the highway was clearest. I would tear past traffic on both the left and the right, passing other cars like they were standing still. When I exited the highway, I raced through the side streets that led to the hospital. I barely stopped the car as I whipped into the emergency room circle. The medical staff rushed out and wheeled Carol through the doors in no time flat. Inside, the intensity written on the faces of all the doctors told me that this trip would be different.

As I watched them tend to her, a sudden, reminiscent sorrow overwhelmed me. It had been many years since I'd felt this particular brand of helplessness, but I remembered it well. As I closed my eyes, my mind drifted back through several decades to when I'd first encountered the feeling.

Dad typically spent his days on sales calls, so when I saw that he'd come home I knew this had to be something serious. My body ached to the point where I couldn't get out of bed. Since I was an active, athletic eleven-year-old, my immobility had been cause enough to ask Dr. Jackson, the family doctor, to make a house call that day.

On that day back in 1956, Dr. Jackson examined me closely as my parents stood by. After he finished, he took my mom and dad into the other room. Their hushed tones confirmed what I'd been fearing: something big was happening. My parents looked crestfallen when they followed the doctor back into my bedroom.

"I'm afraid you have rheumatic fever," the doctor told me. "It most likely developed from an untreated strep throat infection."

My parents explained that they needed to help me get dressed because they were about to call an ambulance.

"The hospital?" I asked. "For how long?"

"We'll see, son," Dr. Jackson said. "At least six weeks. Maybe more."

I furrowed my brow as protest flashed through my mind. "No, sir," I said. "I'm not going to no hospital for any six weeks."

"Look, George," the doctor said with a stern gaze. "Rheumatic fever is nothing to be trifled with. If you overexert yourself, your heart could be in serious trouble. You could even…"

Die. That was what Dr. Jackson clearly wanted to say, but he stopped short—I guess to avoid terrifying a headstrong eleven-year-old kid. Back then, medicine in the US hadn't yet advanced to the point where rheumatic fever could be contained without prolonged bed rest and penicillin. If I failed to follow the doctor's orders, I would find myself at serious risk of heart inflammation, which could result in permanent damage to my heart valves, or even total heart failure.

But my mother knew me well. She had witnessed on countless occasions how stubborn I could be. And I could see from her expression that she intended to side with me.

"If he doesn't want to go, then he isn't going," she declared, cutting off the doctor before he could finish warning me about the dire consequences. Mom stood next to me and squeezed my hand as she flashed a warm smile at the confused physician. "We can take care of it here at home. You just tell me exactly what has to be done."

Dr. Jackson looked at my mother and me, then over to my father, who shrugged in confirmation that he would be of no help in the matter.

"It's important that George avoid any exertion, or it could ruin his heart," the doctor said gravely. "When he needs to get up, you have to help him. And I don't mean that you should help him climb out of bed—I mean that you must carry him wherever he needs to go. I can't stress this enough: He can't exert himself. At all."

Mom was undeterred. "Fine. How long will he need to remain in bed?"

"A minimum of six weeks."

My parents looked like the doctor had just punched them in the gut.

"That's not too bad," I cut in, hoping that the confidence in my tone would perk up my parents. "I can do six weeks in a cinch."

"Well, that's not all," Dr. Jackson added, letting the steam out of my engine. "You have to take his temperature three times a day and record it. He must go two straight weeks without an elevated temperature reading before he even thinks about getting out of bed on his own. This is critically important. If he misses a single temperature reading—even if it's abnormal just once—he has to start all over and begin another two-week testing period."

"Done," my mother replied immediately, and even if she'd felt it, she never showed one second of doubt.

The doctor wrote out the instructions and went on his way.

23

My mom and dad procured a double bed, which they set up in the living room. We never had any money, so I don't know how they managed it or where it came from, but it dominated the leisure space of our little second-floor apartment in Brentwood, Pennsylvania, a neighborhood at the edge of Pittsburgh's city limits. They rearranged what furniture they had and set me up to face our black and white television with nothing more than the three networks the rabbit ears could muster. My dad would make sure that I always had the daily sports page from the newspaper and the latest Sport Illustrated—my favorite magazine as a kid by a long shot.

For the first couple weeks, every day was the same. Mom would get up in the morning and turn on the television while I waited for breakfast. I would eat my breakfast slowly and drink tons of water. I would watch the tube until lunch came, and then I would repeat the process. The same would happen for dinner. Every time I had to go to the bathroom, or got tired of my position on the bed, I would call my mother to help me. My siblings, Barbara, Jimmy, and Tommy, would drop in to say hello after school, but otherwise, I was all alone as the rest of my family went about their lives.

At some point in those initial two weeks, I came across an article about a paralyzed college football player. His family needed help paying the medical bills, so they set up a foundation to accept donations. Right there and then, I knew I had to help. I couldn't move, but I could sure have my mother teach me how to knit a potholder, and that process consumed quite a bit of my time. At first, it was slow going, but within a month's time, I could knit a tight potholder in no time flat. Once I had completed enough of them, Mom helped me sell them to the family and neighbors, and then donate the money to the football player I'd read about.

Apart from that, it was all routine. For the first few days of my time in bed, Mom took the temperatures and marked them down, but eventually, I told her that I could do it. I'm not sure why she decided it would be okay to trust the word of an eleven-year-old, but she agreed. I made a chart of perfect little boxes drawn with a ruler and pencil. Heading the vertical column, I wrote the days of the week, and in the horizontal rows, I listed the times of day when I would take my temperature. Morning, noon, and night, I would record the readings in those meticulous little squares. Over the first few weeks, the temperatures landed all over the place, but then they started to stabilize. Like clockwork, three normal readings would come back to me every day, until I found myself celebrating a full week of perfect results. This continued for the eighth day, then the ninth, and so on.

On day fourteen—the day that would be my last in that bed after weeks of intense boredom—my morning reading turned out to be normal, as well. I only had two more to go. Right before lunch, with great excitement, I put the thermometer under my tongue, closed my eyes, and waited. After a couple minutes, I pulled it out and took the reading. Up one degree. Heartbroken, I double-checked. Then, I repeated the process, hoping that it had been an error. But no. Even after the third try, my temperature was still over by one lousy degree.

This was when, as an eleven-year-old kid, I faced my first real crisis of conscience. I knew I could fudge the number. It wasn't like anyone checked my work. I could just write down a normal reading and then get back to my regular life. Most eleven-year-old kids would do exactly that. And besides, what was one little temperature reading out of the dozens I'd done over the past eleven weeks? Hadn't I suffered enough? Couldn't I be forgiven for moving the goalposts just this once?

Of course I knew the answer. I had no choice. I was an honest kid. Out came the ruler and pencil. I made a new two-week chart and resolved to start the process anew the next morning. My parents were beside themselves about the whole thing. They couldn't believe that I would be willing to subject myself to another long stretch in that bed when I'd come so close to completing the course.

At the end of the thirteenth week, I called my mom into the living room, and she checked the chart. It looked to me like she'd waited up all night in anticipation of the final result. She clearly couldn't wait to call the doctor and get me cleared.

"Well, George did it!" my mother proudly announced into the phone. "Fourteen straight days of perfect readings."

A long pause followed, Mom's expression slowly fading from excited to confused as she turned away from the phone and looked to my dad. "He said that George should get his sneakers on and jog up to the doctor's office," she said, sounding perplexed.

"That can't be right," Dad said. "Ask him again."

So she did. "You want the same kid that's been in bed for over three months to run a mile and half uphill?"

My mother nodded as she listened to the doctor's explanation.

25

When it was done, she shrugged and said she would tell me to get my shoes. Dad seemed less sold by the idea. He watched patiently as I laced up. Then, he trailed me outside and got into his car.

"I'll follow you," he explained. "Just to make sure you're okay."

At the time, we lived in what was then called the Hollows—a section of town below the village of Brentwood. The doctor's office was in the same area that now houses Brentwood Town Square, a steep climb from our home both then and now.

"How ya' feeling, son?" Dad would holler out the window every hundred yards or so.

"Good, Dad, good," I would confirm quickly, motivated as I was to avoid having to return to that bed.

I ran the whole way up the hill, into the building, and straight into the doctor's office. At no point did I feel even remotely exhausted. It was just so exhilarating to be outside again, to use my legs, to draw fresh air into my lungs.

After a thorough checkup, the doctor cleared me to return to my normal activities. I got to be a kid again.

Having been laid up in that bed for over three months, I learned some things about myself. First, I learned that I liked being organized and reaching goals. Also, I learned the power of dedication, that if you committed yourself to something, gave it everything you had, and stayed the course, great things could happen. And even though I was just eleven at the time, I learned what it was like to be bedridden, to need help doing simple things like getting out of bed, and the vulnerabilities such a situation creates. Little did I know then how important those lessons would become decades later, when I would be tasked with helping my dear wife through her own health crisis.

Though Carol had been admitted to the familiar confines of the Stroke Unit at AGH, and though she was under the exceptional care of Dr. Tayal, things had definitely taken a turn for the worse. Dr. Tayal explained that the stroke had reached the basal ganglia area of Carol's brain, which would suppress her communication skills, profoundly impact her balance and movement, and strip away her ability to think before taking an action. On top of that, to avoid further strokes, she would require a blood-thinner for the rest of her life. This would make it more difficult for her blood to clot, and it would send the risks associated with future falls and surgeries soaring.

The damage to her brain threatened to cripple the life that Carol had carved out for herself. Each affected area seemed like a direct attack on the best aspects of her character. Communication skills? Sure, we had our struggles interacting, but she was a great listener. Many nights, when the boys were still young, I would walk in the door from work and find her counseling one of our sons' friends. Plus, talking on the phone was her main connection to her family in Ohio. Balance and movement? She had a whole daily routine that required her to buzz around town in her Jeep Cherokee: stopping by to visit friends, swinging by the grocery store and other errands, and working at the local Penguin bookstore several days a week. Also, it was almost impossible to imagine my wife not being cautious.

On several occasions during the first couple days after her admittance, with this latest damage to her brain causing disorientation and confusion, Carol tried to pull out her various tubes and IVs. After the most recent attempt, the nursing staff outfitted her with a pair of protective gloves to prevent her from continuing the behavior. The gloves made her look like a felled boxer flailing limply at the air. The feeding tube plunging into her throat reminded me that she might never be able to eat on her own again, and that she hadn't said much in the several days since her second stroke.

In a couple of days, she would be undergoing something called a barium swallow test, a critical examination that would determine whether she would ever be able to eat solid foods again or would have to remain on a feeding tube for the rest of her life. I'd seen firsthand from friends and family how quickly life tended to degrade once a feeding tube became permanent, so I left the hospital with a foreboding sense that our future hung in the balance.

I lay awake the rest of the night, pondering how to solve Carol's many new medical issues. She would need so much help, so much care. I vowed to do for her just as my parents had done for me during my bout with rheumatic fever: prepare her food, take her to the bathroom, carry her from place to place, and help her make the best of it. The morning, the day of the swallow test, and the answers to our future couldn't come fast enough. So when the birds started chirping, I sprang out of bed and headed back to the hospital.

Though I knew Dr. Tayal wasn't rounding that day, I figured there had to be at least one doctor there who could answer my long list of questions about the barium swallow test scheduled for the following day. So I headed up to the ninth floor with a warm cup of coffee in my hand and a charge in my step. When I stepped into my wife's room, I met a familiar face. The doctor checking Carol's chart was a neurologist I had known socially for a long time. In the interest of anonymity, I'll call him Dr. Short. Seeing someone I knew helped calm my frayed nerves.

He nodded for me to join him in a conversation outside the room.

"The truth is that Carol's very sick," he told me once we were in the hall. "And she won't live very long."

The blunt force of the statement rendered me unable to speak.

"Sorry, George," the doctor said. Then, he patted my shoulder stiffly and headed down the hall.

A shock of anger rushed through me. *How can you drop a bombshell like that without letting me ask a single question?* But then, the anger was shoved aside by a gut-twisting fear. *How long is not very long?* With a shake of the head, I cleared my mind to avoid the answer to that question, and told myself that this guy had to be wrong. That sense of defiance only lasted for a moment, chased away as it was by the sight of my wife lying in that hospital bed, the reality of all those tubes and wires snaking around and into her.

I found one of the visitors' lounges down the hall. The little alcove was poorly lit. With my face buried in my hands, a memory of our fortieth wedding anniversary came to mind—Carol standing in the crowd of a hundred people and, despite her fear of public speaking, giving a heartfelt and well-delivered speech in honor of the friends and family who'd come. She'd looked healthy and happy that night, chatting with all the guests and laughing at every joke. At the time, I believed that we would breeze past our fiftieth anniversary, and if all the cards fell right, we might even make it to the sixtieth. But the year that had passed since that party felt like a lifetime. And now we faced a new reality, one where Carol's days were severely numbered.

In that small waiting room, I negotiated with anyone or anything that might be listening—an unplanned prayer of sorts—for any extra time I could get. The idea that I might be able to enjoy two more years with her seemed more than reasonable, but also rather abstract. For now, I just wanted her to stay alive for the next hour. Then, a whole day. And after we'd strung together a few days, we could start thinking about weeks.

I sat alone in my kitchen later that night, sipping on an orange vodka and mulling the importance of the swallow test. Just a month ago, Carol had been walking on the beach, and now I couldn't help but fret that she might not live another day without a feeding tube. The looming prospect of another devastating stroke felt like a ticking, unreadable clock hanging over our heads. How much longer would we have together? A year? A month? A day? And how would we spend that time?

Failing the test would be disastrous for anyone's quality of life. But for Carol, it would also mean no more white wine on ice or fountain-poured Diet Cokes, two of her greatest loves. Almost every day over the three decades we'd lived in Sewickley, Carol would drive to the local gas station or bagel shop to get a Diet Coke in a cup filled to the brim with ice. And her bar order of a glass of chardonnay on the rocks had become so predictable that most of the local bartenders would start scooping the ice into the glass the moment they saw us walking through the door. One of my longtime friends had taken to greeting Carol as "Lady Chardonnay."

The pleasure she took in those two simple things was especially unusual for a woman who never much cared about the quality of the food she ate and never spent an overabundance of time on shopping for clothes or jewelry. If she could enjoy a Diet Coke in the afternoon and a glass of wine at night, then she could go to bed entirely content with life. Even though I'd just cleared out all the Diet Coke from our fridge and had vowed to reduce our alcohol intake, I found myself desperately hoping that she would get to enjoy those two great loves again someday. But it all hinged on that barium swallow test—the outcome of which I had no control over.

The next morning, before heading up to Carol's room, I stopped for a quick prayer in the hospital's chapel. Prior to the downturn in Carol's health, it had been a while since I had made a meaningful trip to any house of faith. But I had come up in the old-school way of thinking about these matters, the one that said if you were going to ask God for something, then your butt had better be in a pew. That was why, since the time of Carol's second stroke, just about every Saturday night, right after Communion, you could find me in deal-making mode. The deal was always the same: I'll do whatever it takes to earn more time with Carol. I made this same prayer in the chapel that morning, then headed off to join my wife for one of the biggest moments of her life—and mine, for that matter.

Family members were permitted to watch the procedure through a large glass window. I cringed as Carol refused the test liquid. At first, the technician refused to let me go back into the lab to support her, but I persisted, and he finally relented. I pushed through the heavy lab door and hurried over to my wife. When I got closer, her eyes showed fear, and a depth of vulnerability that cut to my core. The nurses had removed her boxing gloves in advance of the procedure, so I grabbed her hand, which was ice-cold, and held it until it warmed. I told her how important it was to take the test, and asked if she would try. She nodded. Two minutes later, it was done.

As Carol got situated back in her room on the ninth floor, it was clear that the test and the emotions of the day had exhausted her. She was so fatigued that she didn't bother fighting the boxing gloves. Once the nurse had finished securing her and we were alone, I closed the door, slipped off one of the mitts, and held her hand. Carol's grip was so weak, it broke my heart.

Just then, there was a knock on the door. Dr. Tayal and his team had arrived. He assumed his typically kind expression as he addressed us from the end of the bed, and I braced myself to soften the blow of bad news.

"We're going to need to put Carol onto a thickened liquid diet," he said with a sigh.

Since I'd readied myself for the worst news, I had to replay his words in my head just to make sure I hadn't mistaken him. "She doesn't need a full-time feeding tube?" I said, feeling oddly excited about the medically-termed diet I knew nothing about.

"Not for now," he answered in stride. "But any food she consumes must be pureed, and all liquids must be thickened with cornstarch."

I fought the urge to give Dr. Tayal a high-five or a hug.

"Can we thicken wine and Diet Coke?" I asked hopefully, badly needing a win for Carol.

Dr. Tayal measured his response. "We should minimize such things, but yes."

Carol's gaze searched the room in a confused, lost way—and maybe I'd imagined it, but I could have sworn I saw a momentary flicker in her eyes at the thought of returning to her liquid luxuries. When I felt her little hand grab for mine, I scooted my chair in closer to the bed and began combing her hair with my free hand. My wife wouldn't be leaving me that day, the next day, or even the next week. A month or longer still seemed too far ahead to consider, but at least we weren't going hour by hour anymore. Now I could return to my focus of giving her every chance to get stronger and prove Dr. Short wrong about her longevity. We would start by helping her improve her swallowing, day by day. I would make sure that she received the latest and greatest in speech therapy. And once we overcame that, we would move on to the next challenge of relearning how to walk.

Though the irrefutable facts of her brain damage posed potential limits to how high up the hill of health we could climb and what quality of life she could maintain, I was certain I would dedicate my life to maintaining whatever stage she achieved. No matter what condition Carol was in, we would make it work. If we needed to move into a new home to accommodate her disability, we would do it. If I needed to pull away from my job, or retire, I would. And for as long as Carol could stand on two feet, we would continue our life much as we had before. We would still go out to dinner, still find new ways to take vacations, and still create new activities to enjoy together.

Soon after Dr. Tayal left, a nurse arrived with a pureed tomato soup and a cornstarch-thickened cup of water. I found the buttons to move the bed and bring Carol to a seated position. She pointed at the water, so I scooped a spoonful of the grainy gel and fed it to her. Her reaction was to twist her expression and turn away like a toddler who doesn't want her carrots.

Curious, I tried it too. Carol had the right of it. It was an awful, mealy, salty mess. She tried the soup next, which didn't seem to rate quite as bad. I could tell because she looked at the bowl, then at me, and then back at the bowl. I made a note to myself to explore other soup-like meals at the grocery store.

I wanted to encourage her, so I made a big promise. "Someday, you can have as many cold and un-thickened Diet Cokes as you want."

Though she was weak and hushed, and though it was her first full sentence since the second stroke, my wife managed to bowl me over with, "That sounds *so* good."

CHAPTER THREE
unrelenting

Don't give up. Don't ever give up.
– Jimmy Valvano
speaking about his battle with cancer

March 2011

Light poured through the bedroom window. Had I slept in? I whipped around, already knowing that I would see nothing but crumpled sheets in the place where my wife always slept.

"Carol?" I called out.

No response. I rushed into the bathroom and found it empty.

Damn it, Carol. We talked about this. You have to wake me up.

I ran into the long hallway of our new home, relieved that I had installed a baby gate in the entryway heading down to our finished basement. It wasn't possible for her to have tumbled down the steep stairwell.

Finally, I made it to the kitchen, out of breath, and found my wife sitting at the table with a bowl of cereal, a full glass of juice, and one of her ubiquitous magazines. The little countertop television flickered behind her. Having heard me enter, she turned to look back at me.

Instead of following my instinct to sternly remind her that she wasn't supposed to be up and around on her own, I grumbled, "Why didn't you get me up?"

"What's going on?" she deadpanned before turning back to her cereal.

I wanted to laugh, but I knew if I did, it would only encourage her to continue this dangerous behavior. "Jesus, I almost had a heart attack."

She shrugged and went back to her reading. This was a scene I'd encountered thousands of times in my life. It wasn't difficult to drum up the image of her sitting Indian-style at our many kitchen tables over the years, smirking, book in her lap, chin down, engrossed in the

---

Photo: Carol's favorite look, "You have a problem with this?"

33

words, turning the page with one hand and twirling her hair with the other. In those moments, I had often wondered whether Carol preferred her books over me, but this time, as scared as I had been to wake up and find her missing, the sight of her reading gave me great joy.

As I retrieved a coffee cup and a single-serve pod from the cupboard, my heart finally slowed. Carol had come a long way in the nine months since her second stroke. She had progressed to the point where she could make short trips around the house without my help, but it was still imperative that I get up with her in the mornings. The problem was that her balance hadn't fully recovered, and she would trip over her own feet, tumbling to the floor. The fact that she hadn't fallen during the breakfast trapeze performance amazed me.

Much had changed about our lives since Carol's most recent stroke. Shortly after her discharge from the rehab facility, I'd traded our two-story and handicap-unfriendly home for a reverse-ranch-style home in the hills, which allowed us to live on a single floor. Additionally, Carol's mother, Char Perry, passed away. Her father, Stew Perry, had moved in with us. And, I'd finally found some in-home help. Angie, a registered nurse, arrived every morning to check Carol's vitals and blood sugar, work with her on any therapy exercises, and get her ready for the day. As an added benefit, Carol's mornings with Angie gave me a chance to get ahead in my work.

Much had changed about our lives since her most recent stroke. Though she would probably always need caregiving, Carol had made significant advancements. After three challenging months of soupy meals and thickened liquids, she finally passed her barium swallow test. Her hit-or-miss communication persisted, but she had at least started trying to express herself more often, and when she delivered a cogent line, it was often uncharacteristically comedic.

Once, on the way to PNC Park to see a Pittsburgh Pirates game, Carol and I found ourselves in one-lane, bumper-to-bumper traffic because an ambulance had parked in the middle of the right lane. From my perspective, the paramedics appeared to be off duty. Carol wasn't speaking much—she never spoke much during our car rides—so I filled the time grousing as we crawled along. The closer we got, the more I griped about the terrible choice to park an ambulance in a way that choked off a full lane of traffic.

When we finally pulled up next to the ambulance, I caught the driver's gaze. And just then, Carol rolled down the window, turned to me, and calmly asked, "You got anything to say now?"

Frozen with surprise, I said nothing. After the silence hung for a second, Carol rolled the window right back up while staring straight ahead."That was kind of cute," she said, "if I don't mind saying so myself."

I don't think I stopped laughing until the third inning. Her irreverence and comedic timing at that moment had floored me, and it would continue to do so for the next several years.

Though I had come to realize that there would be some permanent disabilities, I felt content in knowing that we were working toward steady improvement. Carol attended physical, occupational, and speech therapy throughout the week, and every month or so we would see some incremental advancement in the speed and length of her steps, and an increasing confidence to speak with authority. Eventually I started to harbor hope that she might at least get close to an independent life.

Her father was a beacon of punctuality and positivity. That morning, Stew came around the corner into the kitchen right at 9 A.M., wearing a wide smile, just like always. As soon as Carol saw him, just as she did every morning, she returned the smile. The two of them had been close for as long as I could remember, a fact I always attributed to how difficult and insulting Carol's mother, Char, had been.

This thought had first occurred to me many years prior. We had just moved to Kent, Ohio, and once our little Ryan-built home was ready, we invited Carol's parents to visit. The minute Char came through the door, she started criticizing everything: the fact that we'd moved to Kent, the placement and choices of the photographs and art on the walls, the dish Carol was using to cook the casserole she'd spent all afternoon preparing, the temperature she'd set the oven, and on and on. It didn't stop for fifteen minutes. Though my wife didn't show it, I could see that the judgments hurt her deeply.

Stew politely waited for the barrage to end, then tried to lift his daughter's spirits with a cheery attitude and gracious words. It was his tactful handling of moments like this that had caused his relationship with his daughter to flourish over the years.

I greatly appreciated his presence in our new situation. He served as a kind of buddy for Carol while also providing me peace of mind that if anything terrible happened while I was in the other room, he would be there to alert me.

Now that Stew had joined his daughter for breakfast, I could get started on my workday. I grabbed my coffee and headed toward the hall. On my way out, I told my father-in-law that he might want to have a talk with his daughter. "She was a bad one this morning," I quipped. "Did you get up without ringing the bell again?" I heard Stew ask her as I hurried downstairs to my office. "What are we going to do with you?"

We had placed diner-style kitchen bells throughout the house, including on the table next to Carol's side of the bed, so she could ring for us if she needed help. She never used them, despite her many promises that she would, until early the following morning when she rang one of the bells for the first time. My anxiety still high after the previous morning's scare, I woke in a hurry and fought through the fatigue to help her with whatever it was she needed.

"Can you get me up?" she asked.

I peeked over at the clock, which read just shy of 4 A.M. We had slept for several hours straight—a small miracle on its own, but what thrilled me most was that finally Carol had remembered to ask for help. Pleased that she'd warned me, I went around the bed and assumed my usual position. I noticed that her Valentine's necklace was in disarray as usual, but since time was of the essence, I figured it could wait until I returned her to bed.

"Okay," I said, anticipating the shift of her weight onto my arm. "One, two, three."

She didn't budge. This was not unexpected, as sometimes she would be fighting her own sleepiness and would take a little longer to respond.

I pressed a little closer to the bed. "Here we go," I said, but she remained a dead weight. "Maybe a little help here?" I quipped.

"I can't get up," she said, sounding like she was somewhere between laughter and tears. "I'm trying."

I bent so low and wrapped my arms around her so tight that we were basically hugging. Without aid, I lifted her. She weighed in at only a little over a hundred pounds, but she was limp as a child in a tantrum, so it took my full strength to pull her to her feet.

"Don't worry," I said. "I'll hold you tight."

I took a step, but she didn't move. She stared at her feet as if to will them to operate, but lost her balance and fell back on the bed.

Oh, dear Lord, I thought grimly. *Please, not another stroke.*

36

Our son Chad had been coming to stay with us from time to time, and he happened to be there that night. I rushed to his room and roused him from sleep. He and I carried Carol to the bathroom. When she was finished, we got her dressed and headed down to Allegheny General Hospital for a CT scan, but not before grabbing my trusty brown bag. I'd learned to be prepared with all the pertinent medical records, the full list of Carol's prescriptions, and a day's worth of pills.

Many hours later, we learned the good news: the scan showed no signs of a stroke. But Carol still struggled to move. I called Dr. Tayal to make an appointment, and he fit us in for later that day.

After calling Carol in from the waiting room, Dr. Tayal watched her intently as she made her way into the examination suite. "How are you?" he asked.

"I'm fine," she replied with a shrug. That was Carol. Always fine. The reply had become something of a mantra, one of her most shining attributes during her waning years.

The doctor glanced at me, and I shook my head.

"I understand you've been having trouble using your legs," the doctor probed.

"Well, I'm fine," she shot back, straight-faced. "That's all I'm saying."

Dr. Tayal's physician's assistant Judy started snickering, which caused me to chuckle as well.

The doctor explained that Carol had a condition known as Vascular Parkinsonism, which occurs with some frequency in a basal ganglia stroke. We learned that the difference between Vascular Parkinsonism and the more commonly known Parkinson's Disease was that while both conditions came with symptoms like slow movement, tremors, difficulty walking, and trouble with balance, Carol's condition would be free of the nerve cell loss typical of Parkinson's. The crushing news was that there was no treatment, and the progressive nature of the disease couldn't be overcome with physical therapy.

"I'm afraid she's going to need a walker or wheelchair to get around," the doctor said. He didn't put it bluntly, but it was clear that, at least in terms of her motor skills development, Carol's progress had ended. Not only would she never get any better with her walking; she would get worse as time wore on.

I felt terrible for Carol, who just couldn't seem to catch a break. I also sensed a creeping resentment about the seemingly endless attacks on my own life. Then I immediately felt guilty as hell for even thinking about myself in such a situation. I forced a smile so Carol wouldn't see the bleak feeling coursing through my body.

"Well, honey," I said with a chuckle, "it looks like you're just going to have to deal with a hunk like me holding your hand wherever we go."

"Whatever," Carol quipped as she rolled her eyes in Judy's direction.

As we worked our way out of the parking garage, I found myself thinking about Hilton Head. In the early 1990s, we had purchased a two-bedroom condo on the island, which back then was still little more than a sleepy golfing destination. But since I was fond of golf and Carol enjoyed the beach, we fell in love with the island immediately. One of Carol's favorite activities in life was to make the trek from our little house in Shipyard to the beach, where she would comb for shells for an hour or two before heading home.

After our youngest son graduated high school, we lived there every winter. Those months down in the low country were some of the best of our marriage. We had the beach, a great group of friends, and an evening ritual that made us quite content. At around happy hour every night, we would take two chairs, a bottle of wine, and our books down to the beach to take in the sunset. Inevitably, we would ignore the books in favor of conversation about our sons or a dreamy retirement. When our sons came to visit, we included them in our five o'clock beach tradition, which always made the evenings even more pleasant than usual.

For obvious reasons, we had missed the season the year after the strokes. Undeterred, Chad and I had taken Carol down for a few days to see how she would manage. Even with our assistance, she struggled mightily to get from the parking lot to the beach. The boardwalk made it easier, but the sand proved impossible to traverse. We wound up having to carry her to the beach chairs. The best shells always lie at the tide's edge, making for something of an uneven minefield for a person with walking issues. So we passed on the idea of searching for shells.

Despite the difficulties, for a time I'd remained confident that Carol would rehabilitate enough to make it possible for us to return to wintering in our favorite place. But this latest turn with her health essentially washed those hopes out to sea.

Before Carol's strokes, my greatest personal pleasures were

working and golfing, mostly because of the routine and social life that both provided. Maintaining my success in my sales region for my current company meant long and focused phone calls or quick trips to visit my salesmen's territories. The time for that had already gotten significantly limited after Carol's strokes, but now with the care related to her Parkinsonism, it was clear that I would have even less time to manage my job, and less contact with the outside world.

Losing the golf would represent a particular challenge, as the hobby had always functioned as my primary form of stress relief and my only source of exercise in recent times. Before the strokes, from April through September, I would work throughout the day, head to the golf course for a few holes of practice, catch up with my friends, enjoy a post-match drink, and then join Carol for dinner. That custom had become my touchstone of happiness.

As we drove from the appointment to complete a list of errands for the day, I tried to give myself a pep talk to drum up some much-needed resolve. Eventually, the perfect source of inspiration came to me. Whether it was as a bed-bound child trying to get two weeks' worth of good temperature readings or as a young man playing to the whistle in every game I ever suited up for, I'd never given up.

Back in 1963, when I was a freshman at Edinboro State College (now Edinboro University of Pennsylvania), all I wanted to do was earn a spot on the basketball team. Even though I was only 5'8" and 135 pounds with shoes on, I knew my fundamentals and hustled more than anyone. In those days, college teams had both freshman and varsity teams, but Edinboro was a Division II basketball program, and so their two teams only had space for scholarship players. I went to tryouts anyhow, but due to my size was never given a chance. So I joined the intramural team.

By midseason, the freshman team had lost two of its players. The head coach had been scouting our league, and he picked a dozen of us to try out. I made the team, and even got into the second half of the first game. That turned into a starting spot just a few games later. By the end of the season, I lettered and was asked to come back on the team the next fall on partial scholarship.

When freshman classes ended, I hurried home to join a semi-pro baseball summer team. Just as our team got going, Edinboro University notified me that I'd failed two classes and needed to go to summer school. Though I hated giving up baseball, I knew I had no other choice if I wanted to get back on the hardwood and continue my education.

I'd flunked English Literature and another course I can no longer recall. Before the summer makeup classes got started, I had to meet with the dean. He informed me that I'd have to get two Bs to be let back in school. I figured the English class would be full of strugglers like me, so I was halfway back to getting that basketball in my hand. Instead, they placed me with eleven eager English majors who were taking their required course before the fall semester. Five minutes into the class, the professor announced that he would be grading on a curve, so to get a B in the course, this meant that I had to beat at least eight other students at Shakespeare. I'd never worked so hard to make a grade. Six weeks later, my expulsion loomed. I requested a meeting with the dean. I had to give it one last shot. My mother had arrived to pick me up and take me home, so she came along.

"Son," he said sternly, "we made a deal and you didn't honor it."

I'd never in my life had to tell my mother I'd failed. I stared at the floor. When it became clear that I couldn't find the words, the dean excused us. Dejected, I followed my mom to the door, but just as I reached the hall, I turned and took a deep breath.

"Can I tell you a story?" I asked.

The dean nodded.

"Sir," I said before I cleared my throat. "You're right. I did make a promise to you."

His gaze followed me as I worked my way closer to his desk.

"But when I made that promise, I couldn't have known that I would be graded on a curve in a class full of English majors. Given another chance, I know I'd pass."

I stood there, tall and proud of my honest and direct pitch. He smiled and stuck out his hand for my papers. I avoided eye contact with my mother, who had to have been confused.

"All right, Shannon," the dean replied. "You're back in, but on academic probation."

"Thanks," I said as I handed him the papers. It was then that I learned a lesson that carried me fifty years in the sales business: know when the deal has closed. Instead of walking out the door, I spoke. "I really appreciate the extra chance, since I really did the best I could."

He looked at me for a long, uncomfortable moment before tearing up my papers. "If that's the absolute best you can do," he said, "then there's no reason to come back." He stood and offered me his hand. "Best of luck to you."

I gave him a strong shake and stood there in shock for a good half-minute.

In the end, my overzealousness with the dean was what got me the boot from Edinboro. Otherwise, I worked as hard as I could to make the team and stay on it, and that mentality had stuck with me for the decades since. Though Carol's medical issues had come hurtling at us at an unrelenting pace, she didn't plan on quitting, and neither did I.

Life for us had already drastically changed, and the difficulty level would soon rise. For years, people I knew had told me I was crazy for trying to take care of my wife in my own home, that a wise man would find the best possible assisted living facility or nursing home and let the professionals handle it. Sure, it would have been easy to give in to the temptation offered in those whispers from friends, and it didn't even seem like it would be a particular indictment of my tenacity. And yet, I never really gave that idea a second thought.

Next, we stopped at Costco for my wife's medicines and some groceries. As usual, Carol was quiet. A sense of loneliness and isolation hung over me. I kept my eye on her as she pushed the shopping cart through the massive discount store. Dr. Tayal had said that as long as her legs would allow, she should continue to use them, and her legs appeared to be doing well. The sight of Carol trucking down those long aisles raised my spirits some. Then it occurred to me that she hadn't seemed depressed even for a moment about the latest medical news. To the contrary, she'd essentially shrugged it off. Tenacious and unwilling to quit, Carol may or may not have grasped the full weight of Dr. Tayal's prognosis, but for today, she moved toward the tall stacks of bottled Diet Coke while she tried to sneak sweets into the cart. She wasn't going to let yet another blow to her health affect her quality of life, and I admired her for this.

It was while standing in the frozen foods section of Costco that I decided I would never willingly place Carol in a home. Perhaps I'd heard echoes of my parents' teachings in my ears, and certainly a good part of me just didn't want to quit. But most of all, I'd made a commitment to this woman, a commitment to be there *in sickness* and in health, and I intended to honor my promise.

The exercise in the store had worn her out, so it took me a while to get Carol back to the car. As we drove the back roads home, I gripped the steering wheel and tried to summon up as much strength as I could and fight off my growing sense of crankiness. I had spent a lifetime teaching my boys not to harbor the woe-is-me attitude, under the belief that it prevented a person from reaching success or true happiness. Yet there I was, feeling sorry for myself over my loss of freedom.

When I got into a mood like this, I knew to be on the alert. A life of self-analysis had taught me it was only a matter of time before someone would do something that I perceived to be wrong, and I would unconsciously drift into that agitated state. In this case, it was that circumstance had robbed me of my carefully planned life of retirement with my wife.

Worry about that later, I told myself, shoving that brewing negativity to the back of my skull.

Just as we pulled into the garage back home, I realized that I had forgotten to cross off an important item on my list. Normally I might have considered leaving Carol with Stew and heading back out on my own, but Chad had taken Stew out for an early dinner."I forgot something in the village," I said as I reopened the garage door and shifted into reverse. Carol had already swung the door open, released the seatbelt, and was turning to get out. "I have to get my purse," she said.

Seriously? I thought, feeling the crabbiness starting to win. Sure, we'd forgotten her purse that morning because we'd left in such a hurry, but the thing was little more than an oversized lipstick-carrier anyway, so what would it matter if she went another twenty minutes without it?

I threw the car back into park and hurried to her side of the car, but Carol seemed like she was trying to do everything possible to make the process of getting her back into the house as difficult as possible. When finally we reached the coat closet, and I helped put the big bag around her shoulder, I apparently did it wrong.

"I hate when you do it like that," she snapped. "I hate it, I hate it."

For a moment, I saw the darkness in my mind perching in the shadows, ready to pounce. I headed for the door, red-faced. Too little, too late. "For Christ's sake!" The words hurled from my mouth before I could tell myself to calm down and swallow my bitter thoughts. But then, one look back at her washed them away in a heartbeat.

"I'm so sorry you have to do all this," she said demurely.

"Do what?" I asked, hating myself for lashing out.

"All this shit," she said, a modern-day Carol-ism if there ever was one. "Taking care of me and having to do everything."

In the instant she spoke the words, all those pesky, lingering, and poisonous thoughts evaporated. I loved her so much at that moment.

"I wouldn't have it any other way," I replied, patting her on the hand.

I led her to her favorite seat in the house, then sat beside her and stroked her hand. The cold truth was that my unwillingness to ever quit, though a good quality, had also put a lot of pressure on me, her, and the whole situation. For too long, I'd been telling myself if/then. If Carol just had some more speech therapy, then she would talk more. If we focused more intently on her therapy exercise, then her legs and balance might come back. And so on. By telling myself these things, I was setting myself up for growing frustration about our lives, her happiness, and my independence. The only "if" I was sure of at this point was that if I kept going at this rate, then I would burn out and likely bring everyone around me down in those flames.

I wanted nothing more than to be a good man to Carol, and to entirely dedicate my life to her. This meant I would have to do something more than just make a promise to be humble. I would have to go beyond not quitting on her. I would need to just be with my wife, embrace the situation, and let life unfold. If I was going to be any good to her, then I would need to find ways to overcome my tendency toward crankiness when things didn't go as I planned.

I went to my office and pulled out the small, black moleskin journal I'd been keeping for years. I popped it open and found a nugget of borrowed wisdom that my past self had left for my future self:

The way out is through it.
– Robert Frost

CHAPTER FOUR
a search for inner peace

If I do not forgive myself for my imperfections
I cannot love myself enough to fully love others.
– Robert Furey, PhD
So I'm Not Perfect: A Psychology of Humility

That near blow-up over Carol's purse deeply concerned me. Instances like it had been becoming more common, but that was the closest I'd felt to losing my cool in a long time. My near loss of control had nothing to do with the small interruption of time it would have taken for me to help Carol fetch her bag. Frankly, it probably would've been wise, since we could've made a pit stop to the restroom. What happened that day was a symptom of something I'd been dealing with my whole life. Though I'd made good on my promise to devote time and energy to taking care of my wife, those old personal demons still lingered.

It's true what they say, that one must take the good with the bad. And that goes for genetics, too. I'd been lucky in so many respects. I had my father's dream-big nature, along with my mother's ability to socialize with anyone. With all that good luck, I suppose I shouldn't have been too surprised that I got saddled with the streak of sensitivity and agitation that ran in my mother's family as well.

My parents both had big families full of people who rarely moved away. At least once a week, my mother's family would swarm to the house that had the most beer. My siblings and I loved going to these gatherings when we were kids because so many of our family's funniest characters would be in attendance. We didn't understand it then, but with those gatherings came a complex web of family dynamics: great stories and big laughter, but also explosive sensitivity and long-held grudges.

Almost every party took a wrong turn along the way, with one family member getting in another's face over some usually

---

Photo: 40th wedding Anniversary in 2009.

inconsequential issue. Something as simple as one person paying a compliment to one family member could cause another to feel aggrieved. The insults would start flying into an argument, quickly marking the end of another gathering.

Each time, as my parents hurried us kids out to the car, I stood in awe of how intense the arguments would become. I can still see how quickly the smiling faces of my aunts and uncles would turn into nasty scowls, how the soft voices would become high pitched, and how they would be sitting one minute but standing and pointing a finger the next. Every time our car pulled away, I would worry that we would never see the family again. That concern would last right up until the following Sunday, when word would invariably get out that someone else was holding a case of beer.

While I'm certain that alcohol played a factor in some of those moments, even as a young kid, I knew there was something deeper. No matter what the issue was, and even though mere time to cool off would have healed all the hurts, it always came down to one of the involved participants needing to set the record straight. Though there was always a high premium on being right, the details of why this was important would usually get lost in the fray.

As I grew into an adult, I began to recognize my own feisty nature, especially when someone disagreed with an idea of mine. I would feel my heart beat a little faster, and a tightness in my chest would wipe away my calm demeanor. My jaw muscles would clench into a grimace, and I would start talking a little faster. Each time, I would hear that little voice in my mind point out how damn wrong the offending party had been, and my lips would part to deliver whatever incredibly astute observation leapt to my mind. But just then, I would muster up the strength to keep my mouth shut. Here's why: I had seen how my family acted with one another, and it scared me to my core. I never wanted to be that way.

Though I learned to put a clamp on it, the heat-up in my mind was inevitable. The one big drawback to this tendency was that the people who offended me never knew how or why they had done so. Instead of seeking confrontation, I would internalize it. My philosophy became, "Keep a lid on it, and it will go away."

Sometimes it worked. I would battle those moments, and the frustration would fade fast. More often, something would happen, and the agitation would fester. During those stretches, my mind would feel like something of a prison. As I went through college and my first handful of jobs, my ability to contain the feistiness weakened.

These episodes only became more frequent after I moved our family back to Pittsburgh and started my own business as an independent sales representative in the architectural coatings industry. One February a few years into that business, it all came to a head. I'd enjoyed some successes, but our overall financial situation was tenuous. I needed every account I could get. So I decided that I would make a trip up to Erie, a small, blue-collar city in the northwestern part of Pennsylvania, to see if I could close some deals. In winter, cloud formations crossing Lake Erie dump blankets of snow on the city, along with frigid snaps of wind. Spending any time outside is a terrible idea. But there's also no better time to visit potential customers who are preparing for major coatings jobs in the spring and early summer.

On that trip in February, despite the success in lining up some meetings, I found myself out of sorts throughout the day. It was nothing specific—just mild agitation—but at the same time, I should have known by then how to read the signs of a feisty streak brewing. With each new interaction with a colleague, I became increasingly annoyed by their attitudes and the tones of their voices.

When I got home that night, nobody in my family seemed to notice. The boys kept to their rooms. Carol was reading. On the stovetop simmered a pot of chili, the third batch in a week. I grumbled my dissatisfaction with the menu choice, but Carol barely looked up from the depths of whatever book she was reading.

"Boys!" I hollered up the stairs. "Come down for dinner." The tone of my voice was what alerted me to my mood. I didn't need a mirror to see that my expression reinforced my irritation. Memories of the bickering at the family parties flooded my mind. So I took a deep breath, grabbed an Irish whiskey, and retreated to the living room.

The sight of my favorite painting, a John Stobart landscape depicting one of the rivers in Pittsburgh in the 1800s, put me in a somber mood. I alternated between stewing and feeling sorry for myself as I slowly finished off the whiskey. Then, with a sigh, I rose from my chair and returned to the kitchen. As I set my empty cocktail glass in the sink, I reminded myself that my mood had nothing to do with my wife, my kids, or even my colleagues. This was just the same internal battle I'd been battling for years.

I awoke the next day and drove to Erie for a series of new

appointments. Some of them broke my way, and some of them didn't. At the end of the day, I stopped by one of my most reliable customers in the hopes of capping the day on a positive note, but he hit me with some upsetting news: another coatings rep was poaching a high-end customer I had been targeting in the eastern Ohio portion of my territory.

The frustration rose to my face, but I buried it quickly in front of my customer. We went on to have a productive meeting, even though I felt the whole time like I couldn't get it over with soon enough. I had to confront this other rep as soon as possible.

The snow was coming down hard and darkness had already set in by the time I hit the road at 4:30. Interstate 79 starts in Erie and runs straight south through a mostly rural landscape until you reach Pittsburgh. The first fifty miles out of Erie have always been quite barren, and I wasn't in the mood for the radio. Instead, I started chewing over the possible interloper in my territory. For that next half-hour, I grinded through his lack of professional courtesy and business ethics.

Who in the hell does this guy think he is? Who does he think I *am?*

My brooding was so deep that I failed to notice the exit signs for Edinboro University, which had never failed to prompt memories of basketball games and lessons learned. A firm grip on the wheel, I started looking for the next rest stop. It was time to call my mentor, Harold Righter, to object to the interference and set the record straight. Harold had run his own coatings agency for twenty years in New England, so I figured he could help.

As I pumped quarters into the payphone, I felt my neck and chest tighten. A roaring headache had started by the time I finished dialing his number.

I didn't even let him say hello before I started in about how this SOB was sneaking into my territory.

"George!" Harold tried to chime in, but I blew past him.

For the next three minutes, I explained how unfair the situation was, how I planned to contact our coatings supplier to raise hell, and how I would demand a meeting with the guy, then get in the car the next morning and drive all the way to Cleveland, where I would catch this turkey in all his lies. When I finally slowed down, a long, quiet moment ensued.

"I can hear you shaking through the phone, George," Harold said in his thick Boston accent.

The words snapped me back to reality. I hung up the phone without saying goodbye. Then I returned to my car and leaned back onto the hood. The last bit of light was fading over the trees to my right. The wind had picked up. Images of my temperamental family flashed through my mind. I closed my eyes and thought of my wife and three boys. From the ash tray in my car, I grabbed a couple more quarters, then returned to the payphone. I had to do something about this. I couldn't wage this battle alone anymore.

A familiar and loving voice answered on the other end of the line.

"Dad," I said with a sigh. "What was the name of the retreat you used to go to in the city?"

St. Paul's Catholic Church and Monastery sat high on a bluff overlooking Pittsburgh's historic Southside neighborhood. As I came upon the iron gate at the outer edge of the notable church, I felt equal parts excited and anxious. A few members of my family, like my dad, had long encouraged me to attend as they saw the troubles in me well before I did. So there I was, like my father and uncle before me, waiting for the bell to ring to begin the weekend.

Having arrived a few minutes early, I decided to pass the time with a stroll through the grounds. I reached the garden and breathed in the beautiful view of Pittsburgh.

I began to feel silly. When was the last time I'd been to church and meant it? How would I plan to find peace here? And why was I being so hard on myself? I had led a successful life. I was married to an adorable and easygoing wife, and I had three good sons. I owned my own house and ran my business from an office less than a mile from where I lived. I was forty-five years old, and everything was going my way. Sure, just beneath the surface, I'd battled with that agitated self, but apart from my occasional crankiness, I rarely acted out. I figured I'd find a way to ignore the inner turmoil and headed for the gate and back to my car.

When I was halfway back to the gate, the St. Paul's church bell rang, freezing me in my path. I'm not sure if it was Catholic guilt, a sense of obligation, or the fact that the sound also meant dinner was ready, but I turned around to join the group heading for the cafeteria. A short Mass followed, after which we learned that we would be on our own for the rest of the night. There was no whiskey or wine, or any other libations. No TV or radio, either, and I hadn't brought anything to read. I was totally out of my element.

Right then, as if by cosmic reminder, I was paged to the reception area, where I picked up the phone sitting on the desk. My good friend Joe Curtin was on the other end of the line.

"George Shannon at a church retreat," he said. "This is sacrilegious."

"I'm trying to do something good in my life," I replied.

He laughed. "When Carol told me you were there, I had to call and confirm it for myself. I'll be at Froggy's tonight if you change your mind." I shouldn't have been surprised. I was always one of the guys. Always having a good time. And I certainly understood why none of my friends could believe that I'd cloister myself in a seminary over a weekend, trying to make myself a better person.

After hanging up with Joe, my instinct was to find someone to chat up, but I fought that urge and wandered into the seminary library and sat down. The quiet of the room made me uncomfortable. Though back then I'd never have understood why, it has become very clear that the total lack of distraction forced me to face the uncomfortable: true self-reflection. I'd convinced myself up to this point that taking control of my life and striving for perfection had been the tools I needed to achieve happiness, but instead I'd been feeling worse. In those painfully quiet moments, I resolved to change, but I had no idea how. As I waited for an answer, it occurred to me that I was sitting among hundreds of books—spiritual ones no less.

I knew my reading tendencies, so I figured I would need to find a smaller book. I paced up and down the aisle until a thinner, black-bound title jumped out at me: *So I'm Not Perfect: A Psychology of Humility,* by Robert J. Furey, PhD. I read the first few paragraphs and was immediately gripped. For the next hour, I sat on the leather chair in the library, soaking up one nugget of insight after another. It was as if this book had been written directly to me. Each passage seemed to reveal something new that would absolutely floor me.

When I glanced at the library clock, I discovered how late it had become, and realized I had to get to my assigned bunk for the night. Though I'd seen the sign that asked visitors to leave the books in the library I wanted neither to stop reading nor risk having another self-reflective soul getting their hands on these one hundred fifty pages of wisdom. I scanned to make sure nobody was around and palmed the book to my side like I was sneaking out top secrets. Since I planned on returning the book at the end of the weekend, I figured no sins had been committed.

The minute I returned to my room, I pulled out a little black notebook in which I'd been keeping some personal observations as well as any inspirational quotes I'd heard or come across. I found a page in the Dr. Furey book I'd earmarked and transcribed the passage word for word into my notebook:

"Without humility, pride becomes conceit and arrogance."

And then I read that wonderful sentence again and again. Those eight words shot through my mind, shining a bright light on my behavior of late and beyond. I didn't have a full grasp of the concept of humility then, but I knew one thing, that I had to stop always wanting things to be my way or needing things to be perfect. So what if Carol had made three batches of chili in one week? Was she loyal? Yes. Was she taking care of the house like we'd agreed upon? Check. Had she done her part to raise our kids as independent young men as we planned? Yep.

The truth was, I owed it to her. She always bore the brunt of my self-important streak. Just as I had convinced myself that in striving for perfection, I was only trying to be successful in business, that faulty belief had served as something of a trap for my marriage in my many attempts to "help" her. It wasn't a failure to get my way that always triggered me. That was just a symptom of my problem. To overcome, I would have to start seeing things for how they were, rather than for how I thought they should be or imposing my own version of what ought to be.

I should have known better; I'd seen my family bicker over a hundred little injustices that were likely created out of their own minds. What would I accomplish if I drove to eastern Ohio and gave that coatings rep a piece of my mind? Nothing, and frankly it would've been an act of selfishness. It all made so much sense. Immediately, I realized that I needed to be more tolerant. It was, after all, that same desire for tolerance that had caused me to enroll in this retreat in the first place. Perhaps I could sit down with the guy and figure out ways to make both of our agencies better. If not, at least I tried.

To me, humility meant thinking of others more than I had been, and that's what I intended to do. I spent the rest of the weekend sneaking back to my room and jotting down every last one of my favorite passages of wisdom.

I left that wonderful retreat full of energy and hope for the future. When I got home, I went to the local bookstore and ordered a handful of copies of *So I'm Not Perfect*. I made my peace with the encroacher from eastern Ohio. I became more tolerant of others in my workplace. I found ways of introducing new meal ideas to Carol and tried to enjoy my kids' busy lives as best I could. I couldn't have been happier that first month. Right around that point, I ran into an old friend and shared my awesome experience with him. He smiled and bluntly, though politely, told me it wouldn't last. I blew it off and ignored his comments. It turned out he was right; six months later, I'd fallen back into my normal patterns: delving deep into work, building and maintaining impeccable landscaping at my home, and losing my tolerance and humility.

The truth was that the more I asserted myself in life, the better I felt. To see order and neatness in my world felt comforting. In those times, the confrontational thoughts would stay mostly in the background, a quiet but constant murmur. When life got messy, literally or figuratively, those tenaciously righteous thoughts would demand to be heard, and I would battle them with all my might before eventually winning the day. I figured that the idea of inner peace was something like a mirage, just something pleasing to ponder but never all that attainable. I assumed someone like me would never find true happiness and come to terms with that truth. There are few moments I can remember in life where I am more grateful to have been wrong.

[A humble man] will not be thinking about humility:
he will not be thinking about himself at all.

– C.S. Lewis
Mere Christianity

CHAPTER FIVE
the healing power of humility

By December of 2012, I'd been taking care of my wife for a little over two years. I had approached her new health situation like I had everything else since I was a child: head-on. I learned everything I could about her condition, discovered ways to improve her health, and provided those opportunities, all while keeping things organized and on track. My unwillingness to quit was something I could finally put to good use. Trying to make Carol's situation the best I could had created an unexpected happiness and sense of fulfillment. I began to think that my purpose in life had become clear.

Unfortunately, over the years, my inner dialogue had evolved cleverer and cleverer ways to undermine any happiness I ever managed to find. Even now, it was exhibiting its craftiness on my newly discovered sense of peace. I soon became frustrated by the lack of options to improve Carol's health, and it seemed to me that suddenly even the aspects I had mastered—like keeping her diabetes under control—became quite unpredictable. A bad sugar reading would feel like a failure on my part, and this would send my thoughts down a road toward crankiness and negativity.

No matter how hard I tried, I couldn't make Carol better. If my very purpose for living was to take care of my wife, then the chatter in my mind always had the means to twist the knife. I feared that eventually my demons would win.

That was my somewhat brittle mental state at the time I received the call.

"I'm sorry, George," came the news, "but the treatments weren't effective. You still have cancer."

I had been diagnosed with prostate cancer at a time when the dust had barely settled on my sixtieth birthday. Carol was still healthy then. My oncologist recommended that we forgo any radiation treatment and instead go straight to surgery to remove my prostate. Follow-up tests showed that the surgery had failed to deliver me a perfectly clean

Photo: With friends Robert E. McCarthy Jr., Janet McCarthy, Linda Hoehl, and Greg Hoehl.

bill of health. A small amount of detectable cancer matter remained in my prostate bed. At the doctor's recommendation, we made the decision to wait on radiation treatment, based on my relatively young age and the likely side effects. I submitted to regular checkups and blood tests, and we started radiation at what the doctor felt was the appropriate juncture.

But now I sat there dumbfounded with the phone in my hand, having learned the hard way that we'd missed the appropriate juncture. That's a difficult enough thing to hear on its own, but the worst part was that I didn't even hear it from my doctor. The call had come from his secretary. The inner boil spilled over in an instant.

What kind of doctor has his secretary do his dirty work? This is cancer, for Christ's sake.

As soon as I managed to collect myself, I called the doctor directly. "Tell me what these results mean," I said, trying to keep a level tone.

"It means you'll never be cancer-free," he said flatly.

When I heard those words, it took every stitch of what I had to fight against my anger. Many years of taming down that predisposed agitation of mine went to tatters in an instant. Though I wanted to take him to task for not calling in the first place, I got off the phone without incident.

I won the immediate battle in my mind with that doctor, but the rest of my day was full of sour thoughts as I ruminated on how I had just learned that, like my wife, I would spend the rest of my life battling a terminal condition.

A couple weeks went by, and the bitterness in my mind only grew as I sat alone with my pain. Within a month, I reached a breaking point. One night, my son Chad stopped by unexpectedly and found me sitting gloomily in the dark. He tried to cheer me up by staying with me for a couple hours and discussing the situation, but it was no use.

The somewhat embarrassing experience left me with the feeling that I needed to do something about my dark mood. The next morning, I went to my office to see if I still had any copies left of that wonderful little book about humility I'd read twenty years prior. Once I opened the book, it was as if I'd never left the quiet confines of the church library.

I reread the passage about how arrogance grows in the absence of humility. In my younger days, I must have missed the basic meaning behind that critical observation: unless you can remove yourself from the center of your universe, you will suffer from being at the center of your universe. To be humble is to break down the energy-sucking ego that can never be satisfied. I had spent a large part of my life battling with my own tendencies to seek out the imperfections, whether that meant obsessing over the details in my business environment or being hard on Carol because she hadn't done things the way I preferred.

All my life, I had convinced myself that taking charge was a virtue, and it certainly served its purpose of helping me building my business and therefore providing for my family. That tactic required that I put me first. Yes, it gave me the strength to see anything through, including the goal of caring for my ailing wife, but it also originally stemmed from a desire to serve my world, my needs, and my ego. I still hadn't let go of my goal of getting her healthy again, and had been banking my hopes on the idea that she was going to get better. My goals and expectations weren't being met, which had given rise to the kind of gloominess that made me forget my place.

If I was going to last in the face of cancer and a progressively ailing wife, I needed to find a new path. The question then arose as to which route to take. I kept reading, and when I came across the words, I remembered them as clear as the day I'd jotted them in my notebook many years prior.

"Our very first problem is to accept our present circumstances as they are, ourselves as we are, and the people about us as they are."

There were no more fixes, but acceptance does not equal quitting. Like a fog lifting, it became wildly clear to me. My never-quit mentality had fed the chatter in my mind and thus prevented me from possessing true clarity regarding my situation. I sat down in my office chair and sighed, a long breath of both relief and sadness. It felt good to shed the burden of trying to fix everything and keep my life in perfect order. And the grief that overcame me arose from the realization that my wife and I were sick. I scanned my office walls with all the pictures of my family and awards in business. Time was moving fast, and our lives on this earth were limited.

My mind became still, perhaps for the first time in my life, but certainly for the first time in the last two decades. *Accept the cancer. Accept me. Accept Carol. Accept the world around me.* The next few moments were as exhilarating as I'd ever experienced. Ever since Carol's strokes, I'd been saying that I wanted to make her feel the love, but for the first time, that phrase made sense. It was about more than being a reliable husband or stepping up to the initial challenge of her disability. I wanted to make my life about her, all about her, for the rest of her life—or mine, if that was the case. To be a vessel for her happiness, fulfillment, and enjoyment of her life.

Cancer was a difficult prospect, but I couldn't change it. In some ways, it made my desire to be fully selfless more intense. If I was destined to die before Carol, then I wanted to make sure I went down having given her everything I had. The thought that I would get to spend the sunset phase of my life with my one-of-a-kind wife made me feel almost giddy in that moment.

Before closing the book that day, I found one more critical lesson: "If I do not allow for my own imperfection, I will never really know myself."

It wouldn't be easy. Life would throw me curveballs and some days would be quite difficult. If I lost sight of this truth, I would slip back into the same patterns and allow my old self to rule the day. Remembering my own imperfection would be the compass to guide the rest of my journey. From this moment on, these became the words I called on whenever I needed to identify my true north.

A few months later, I would face a major test. One of my oldest friends put me on to a cancer doctor named Dave Parda. When I first met with Dr. Parda, he explained we could make one last-ditch effort, a radiation laser-focused blast at the tumor site, and with this strategy came a glimmer of hope. Dr. Parda's team spent many sessions with me, fine-tuning their blast location based on my anatomical measurements and the assistance of high-end computing. I found myself thinking that maybe we'd beat this thing after all.

The following week, the radiation went off without a hitch. But the subsequent meeting with Dr. Parda didn't deliver the best news. Despite the perfect precision, the zap of radiation had stunned the tumor into submission, but hadn't destroyed it. The short of it was that my cancer would never be cured, and our next step would be to find ways to manage the slow-growing disease. We'd start hormone therapy soon and eventually move on to chemotherapy.

Now, considering I'd gotten my hopes up, I'll be the first to admit that I expected a wave of anger to destroy me in that moment, but it never came. As I left the cancer center and got in my car, I waited for the swirling thoughts of injustice to clutter my mind, but they failed to appear. Instead, I found myself thinking about the practical implications of taking care of Carol during chemo treatments. Driving down the highway, I took the quiet time to check for lurking demons of old, but my search turned up empty.

My relationship with Carol had flourished as of late. Though we had normal marital challenges, life had been so much more interesting. We'd been having such fun and so many laughs, and had spent more time together in that period than we had in the whole of the decade prior. I didn't want news of a terminal illness to ruin all that, so I decided I'd downplay it with her. When I entered our front door, I found my wife in her usual spot in her chair, her tiny legs propped up on the ottoman, a magazine in her lap as she brushed her lips with a business reply card in the way that always soothed her.

Her eyes met mine. "Oh, there he is," she said, as she often did when eager to see me.

I marched straight to her and gave her a long hug, and the mantra crossed my mind as naturally as the blood flowed from my heart: *Accept me, accept her, and all your circumstances.*

I really should have expected the blunt question that followed.

"Are you going to die or something?"

Some younger version of myself would have jumped all over that remark as being less than tactful. Instead, I focused on how much I enjoyed her offbeat and frank manner.

"I'll be with you for all your days," I whispered in her ear. "All your days. Do you understand?"

A year or so later, I elected to undergo a new chemotherapy treatment, which rendered me physically useless and bound to the couch.

After a chemo treatment, I felt the absolute worst, like a toothache and the worst flu had simultaneously invaded every fiber of my body. As I sat on the living room couch, wishing nothing more than to be able to curl up and go to sleep for the next three days, I glanced over at Carol. She must have sensed my attention on her, as she looked away from Doctor Oz on TV.

"Why don't you try to sleep?" she asked.

Restlessly, she wiggled about in her chair while glancing at me every few seconds. I had learned that this jumpiness meant Carol was feeling like a burden, but it went beyond that. She wanted to be an active part of our lives together. She wanted to do something for us, take care of things for a while, and just be her own person. She wanted to water and prune her orchids, swing by her favorite store to buy some thoughtful cards for family and friends, or even just make her own peanut butter toast for breakfast. These were the times I felt the worst for Carol.

"I'm okay," I said, stretching the truth beyond recognition. "Just need to rest my feet a little while."

She gave me one of her patented headshakes with a little shoulder shrug, a move that translated directly as "I know you're bullshitting me, but what else can I do?" She kept her eyes locked on me as I battled that coveted sleep. I must have dozed for a moment, because the next thing I knew, Carol had worked her way up on the walker and moved a few feet away from the chair. Instead of making her customary left down the hall in the direction of the bathroom, she went straight into the kitchen toward the refrigerator.

"Whatcha' doing, honey?"

"Making you lunch," she replied loudly. "You got a problem with that?" She turned around to stare me down.

For a split second, I considered telling her not to worry. Instead, I just chuckled at the stern delivery. I also remembered how important it had been for her to take care of me when I was first diagnosed with this disease a decade ago. So I forced my weary body up from the couch and stood near her in case she lost her balance. Other than having me grab the plates from an unreachable shelf, she did the rest. In about ten minutes, we both had American cheese sandwiches with mustard, and we split a Diet Coke.

When we finished, Carol scooted herself back to her chair while I trudged through the full list of tasks and household chores that needed to be done. An hour or so later, and running on empty, I flopped down on the couch. Though I wanted to, out of my own fear for my wife's wellbeing, I couldn't let myself fall asleep. I had noticed that Carol was fidgeting with the newspaper, and I knew what she wanted.

"Anything good in there?"

"I want to see all of them," she replied. "Do you want to pick?"

I rolled off the couch, grabbed the movie section of the paper, and picked one for later in the afternoon. Sure, the pain would be unbearable, but making every day of Carol's life the best day of her life had become the thing that gave me the most happiness, the thing that made me feel at peace with myself. Not even the misery caused by chemo could take the value of that away from me. After all, I didn't know how many more days I would get.

Was our life perfect from then on? Certainly not. The big difference after that day I first picked up *So I'm Not Perfect* during my retreat in the 90s was that I had accepted my own faults and could finally love myself enough to make my love available to my wife in a way we had never reached before. This gave me the chance to know her—and us—in a whole new light.

That was how I learned to smile instead of being angry, be kind over confrontational, and humble over self-righteous. My old inner self still knocked on the door a dozen times a day, but my understanding of what humility required gave me the edge to refuse entry. When I made mistakes, I apologized. If I felt like I was losing the battle, I picked up my notes and reviewed them. I reminded myself that life, even at its best, would never be perfect, but the key was to accept it on its own terms.

CHAPTER SIX
better days

We are not the same persons this year as last; nor
are those we love. It is a happy chance if we,
changing, continue to love a changed person.
– W. Somerset Maugham
The Summing Up

Even though I'd been a fan of the University of Pittsburgh's football team as a kid, I'd always thought of Notre Dame as a nearly mystical place. Maybe I'd fallen for the Knute Rockne story. Whatever the case, it was 1967, and Joe Curtin, a good friend from high school, had made Pitt's team as a defensive back. When I heard he'd moved up to the starting job, it made the annual matchup with Notre Dame seem even more exciting. I circled the day on the calendar: Saturday, November 11th, and made sure I got the time off from my job in Youngstown, where I was working my way through college at the time.

I arrived home that Friday night in enough time to catch a drink with another high school buddy, Tommy Ryan, at a local pizza parlor called Pinchero's. The moment we opened the door to the restaurant, I spotted that easy smile of the woman I would come to love. On either side of my future wife sat a pair of her friends, Linda and Janet. This trio would remain the best of friends for decades after.

But in the meantime, I only had eyes for the girl in the center. Carol Perry didn't seem like she had a care in the world. This attitude permeated everything she did, from the way she held her cigarette to the way she laughed so easily. Tommy introduced us, and we talked about everything from my fascination with Bobby Kennedy to our dreams in life, and even to my uncertainty about what I would do after graduating from college. Mostly we laughed for the next few hours. In her quiet but attentive way, she made me feel like the most important person in the room, or in all of Pittsburgh, for that matter. As we got up to leave, she stood as well. That was when I first noticed that Carol couldn't have been a centimeter taller than five feet. She was the most

Photo: Wedding day, March 15, 1969

63

adorable thing I'd ever seen. Just as I was about to go, I felt a tug on my sleeve. Carol had written her phone number on a slip of paper, and was reaching out to hand it to me. With a grin, I took it and left.

"Watch out," Tommy said once we'd gotten out to the parking lot. "That Perry girl is looking for the hoop."

My friend's assessment was on the money, but neither of us could have figured that I would soon be willing to oblige.

Carol and I dated for just under a year. The rare times I made it back to Brentwood, I would take her for a bite to eat, and we would invariably end up at one of our families' houses. When we went to her house, we would quietly watch television with her parents. But Carol preferred to spend time at my family's parties, where drinking, teasing, and dancing were always the order of the night.

One weekend, I was home from Youngstown to visit her. Between finishing up my senior year and my full-time job at the bank, these visits were painfully few and far between. Just a couple months earlier, I'd made our relationship a lot more official by giving her a lavalier, a necklace bearing my fraternity's name. She'd been so excited that she flashed that beautiful smile of hers everywhere we went.

On this occasion, the last night home before heading back to school, I picked Carol up in my black Chevy Camaro—I was so proud of that car—and took her on a date. We were heading to South Hills Village, a new mall, when we pulled up to a stoplight at one of the main intersections in town. I was bobbing my head to the radio and keeping an eye on the red light when she turned to me and blinked her big blue eyes. I braced myself, because she'd never really looked at me quite so theatrically.

"So," she said, "are we going to get married or what?"

The truth was that I was enamored with Carol, but hadn't been thinking about marriage just yet because distance had prevented us from spending much time together in the eleven months since we'd first met. Given that I was someone who'd led an almost entirely practical life up to that point, my reply surprised even me.

"Yes," I said. "Let's get married."

When the light turned green, we drove off and spent the rest of the night celebrating.

We wasted no time setting the date: March 15, 1969. In those days, weddings were relatively simple affairs. The one stipulation I asked for was to get married at the Catholic church I'd grown up in, St.

Sylvester's in Brentwood. We had our reception in the banquet hall of a little mom and pop hotel nearby. My extended family was enormous, so it felt almost more like a Shannon/Kramer reunion than a wedding.

At some point later into the night, I finally had the chance to dance with my new wife. She looked so beautiful in her dress. I remember thinking how crazy it was that I'd married this woman just eighteen months after meeting her. But the longer we danced, the more that feeling gave way to a sense that Carol was the one for me, and that someday soon we would start a family.

When it was time for us to leave the reception, my brother Jim brought the car around for us. My Uncle Charlie, truly one of the silliest people to have ever lived, waited for Carol to climb into the car before he jumped into the driver's seat and sped away without me. The crowd went wild. Fifteen minutes later, he returned my car and new wife to me. I can only imagine how he must have teased her during that ride.

As he was handing me the keys, he grabbed me and said loud enough for everyone to hear, "Hey, kid. She's a real keeper, so don't mess it up."

Everyone got a good laugh at that one. When I hopped in the car, I was met by the same smile that caught my attention in the pizza parlor. I told her I would keep my promise, and she kissed me.

As we made our way to the Pennsylvania Turnpike, my new wife tallied up the wedding envelope proceeds, so we could figure out how many honeymoon days we could afford. The location had been my choice. Long in love with American history and intrigued by government, I wanted to see everything Washington DC had to offer, and Carol went right along with me. For three straight days, I took her to one historical site after another. Though the constant movement clearly exhausted her, Carol kept on trudging at my side.

Toward the end of the trip, she indulged me one last time. I couldn't leave the city without seeing Ford's Theatre. I've always been fascinated by the Civil War. Imagine my heartbreak when we found that while the museum was open, the theater itself was closed. The entrance had been covered by a makeshift door marked with a sign reading "under renovation." Undeterred, I pulled back the plywood barrier just enough for Carol and me to slide in before letting it clap shut behind us.

Alone in that theater, I grabbed my wife's hand and led the way to the spot where John Wilkes Boothe had spied on Lincoln. The whole way up, she voiced her concerns about getting caught. But when we looked through the peephole that Boothe had made, she seemed to become just as enthralled as I was. Hand in hand, we ventured into the viewing booth where Lincoln had watched the play, and we finished by sitting in the very same seat where the president had passed his last moments.

Our time in Ford's Theatre was like a microcosm of our life together. I had always been willing to race after what I wanted, and Carol had always chosen to come along, open and accepting of whatever our newest adventure might bring. Now, some forty-plus years later, it was my wife's needs that dictated the day's journey, and I'd become the willing participant.

September 2016

The living room clock read 7:00 A.M. The last time I'd peeked in on Carol, right after my quick read of the morning paper, she'd been snoring away. So I settled into my desk chair, second cup of coffee in hand. The next sixty minutes would be the only stretch in the day that belonged to me alone. I clicked my desk lamp on low and tucked into the beautiful silence. Every extra minute that Carol slept in the morning would make her day better. The correlation was remarkable. If she slept well, we almost always would have an incident-free day. But if she woke early, something troublesome would happen. Perhaps she would be more fatigued than usual and take a tumble on the way to the car, or something in her metabolism would be off, sending her into a low blood sugar state. Whatever the case, more sleep meant fewer problems.

As Carol slept, I checked my calendar for appointments, grabbed a pen and notepad, and started a list. Fifteen minutes later, I had assembled a game plan for the day. Predictably, the dishwasher beeped. I emptied it with an almost comic dedication to quiet, then moved on to Carol's morning setup. I set out a glass of water, a *USA Today* reassembled with the Life section on top, an array of her pills, a placemat, a spoon, and a bowl of dry cereal. I would wait until she reached the counter to add her almond milk—a necessity because of her lactose intolerance. Next to her breakfast, I placed her glucometer, which we would use to test her morning blood sugar levels. Finally came the tissue we would use to wipe off the drop of blood that would follow pricking her finger with the glucometer's needle.

I drifted back to my computer to glance at the video monitor that allowed me to keep an eye on Carol while tending the morning tasks. The only change since last I checked the monitor was that she had flipped from facing the window to facing the bathroom side of the bed. I knew I would have about fifteen minutes until she tried her daily morning escape to the bathroom without telling me.

I gazed through the monitor at my wife, tucked cozily into a ball of comforter and sheets in the dark bedroom. Since the second stroke, I had thought of Carol like a little injured bird I was keeping safe in the palm of my hand. I hadn't always held such a tender view of our relationship. In fact, there had been a series of losing battles in our marriage when I had tried to change Carol, or to make her think differently about things, or maybe to just convince her to hold stronger opinions or take more charge of the life we shared.

Before we got married, I tried my hand at teaching middle school kids. While I had a few memorable moments—like when my class wrote me personal notes after Bobby Kennedy was killed—education was a profession for which I found myself ill suited. Then, a few months after Carol and I tied the knot came one of the shortest military service stints in the history of the Marines. I'd been excited about the chance to serve my country, but two weeks into basic training, they discovered my heart murmur and issued me an honorable discharge. Uncertain of what to do next, I applied for a series of sales jobs and landed one with Koppers Inc. The only trouble with this new job was that we would have to transfer to Minnesota in the dead of winter. Despite the fact that Carol worked at TWA, a job she loved to death, and that we would have to move away from our families, Carol proved totally fine with the move.

It didn't take long for us to become unhappy in the Great White North. I was new to sales, and I had zero direction at work, hated the cold, and missed my family. Carol struggled to adjust to life away from Pittsburgh as well. But when I asked her what she wanted to do next, she claimed that it didn't matter. This irritated me, as I wanted her to participate in the decision-making process, or at least share some insight. But instead, I got nothing. We moved five times in the next seven years, and each time, I felt like the decision rested solely on my shoulders, as Carol claimed that she would be fine anywhere.

Perhaps my feeling that we had merely been spouses and not partners in our marriage went way back to the beginning.

The way I'd seen it back then, this was just one of the many signs of Carol's lack of initiative. Whether the matter was as trivial as choosing a vacation destination or as serious as finally following through on confronting her overbearing mother, she never showed much interest in sharing her opinion. I had always figured I could change that. I was wrong, but she did have a quiet way of doing things on her terms, even as she went with the flow. I just failed to see this wonderful attribute, or better yet *accept* this until much later in our marriage.

The gentle tone signifying the end of the dryer cycle called me to our laundry room to begin the process of gathering and folding a load of warm towels.

Just as I finished folding the towels and setting them on my desk in the living area, the ring of the landline phone carved through the blissful silence. The loud intrusion into Carol's best moments of sleep forced a cringe. Caller ID announced that it was the local pharmacy calling to notify that the next batch of medicine was ready for pickup. Another item to add to the day's list.

I placed the phone back into the cradle and, out of instinct, turned to the monitor. Carol had those Tweety legs pointed straight up in the air, and the slowest escape in the history of mankind was underway. I pulled the door open, the soft living room light casting into the room.

"Oh, shit," Carol muttered, caught in the act yet again.

"Where were you going, buster?"

"Were you spying on me again? I hate when you do that."

Truth be told, I hated the necessity of it, too, but what could I do? Carol's condition had regressed to the point where she was far less capable of guarding against poor choices. The minute I would look away, she would be off trying to walk on her own, and she just wasn't capable of that anymore. Even so, I couldn't blame her for the desire. Imagine what it must feel like to be under constant supervision.

Before the strokes, Carol had enjoyed a life all her own. She had once co-owned with her good friend Mareena a customized gift store called Perfect Presents. Carol had loved that little business and wished it had lasted longer. She often mentioned fond memories of how our boys would visit her at the store's location in the village. At least once a week, Chad, who has always had a sweet tooth, would hit her up for one of the fancy chocolate bars she used for gifts.

As our kids grew older, Carol clerked at the local Penguin bookstore and worked part-time for a florist, helping with the arrangements. She would also spend one Monday a month at the women's shelter in downtown Pittsburgh. In the last few years before her life took that drastic change, she volunteered a few days a week at the hospital just up the street from the center of town.

For someone like Carol, that sense that she was always being watched and that she had lost any real measure of independence must have been frustrating.

I went to the bed and helped her to her feet. "Maybe I just couldn't wait to see my honey."

"That's a good one," she replied. "Is she here yet?"

I chuckled. "You've got me today."

"Oh, Christ."

One thing that always struck me about Carol was that she could deliver more emotion in those two words than most inspirational speeches I'd ever heard. In this case, she was conveying her preference to be bathed by Jennifer, whose bathing technique far surpassed her husband's "hosing down" approach. Several mornings a week, Jennifer, who was a certified nursing assistant, would come over and help with Carol's morning care. As part of the routine, she would apply lotion that would leave Carol smelling like some kind of exotic flower. Of course my wife cared little about the lotion's scent. What she was after was the massage-like experience of the application. This luxurious routine was one of the many reasons that Jennifer would become one of Carol's closest friends in the last few years of her life.

After helping Carol to the bathroom, I had just enough time to make the bed and fetch the folded towels I had left on my desk. Like clockwork, I found her standing in the doorway of the bathroom right when I returned. Just like every day, we lumbered slowly and steadily off to the kitchen. As we passed the stack of towels, Carol reached out and patted them, almost as if to thank me for doing the laundry.

"Look at that," she said, delighted at the sight of the array I had prepared for her on the counter. "It's all ready for me. Thank you." Carol made this same observation every day as if she had never seen the spread before.

I helped her to her seat, then applied the glucometer to the finger she held up reflexively. With her free hand, she'd already started leafing through the Life section of the paper. The glucometer returned

"121," a good number. With a healthy blood sugar reading and a sound few hours of sleep, this felt like it would be a good day.

The pills went down without a hitch, which was also a good sign, because Carol's stiff esophagus typically made for a struggle with the bigger ones. I poured the almond milk. The oven clock read 8:15. This left us half an hour—along with sufficient contingency time for the inevitable surprise or hurdle that each day presented—before I would need to help Carol brush her teeth and then get her in the bath. If all went well, we would make it to her first doctor's appointment at 10 o'clock with plenty of time to spare.

She would need every bit of that thirty minutes to eat her bowl of Puffins Peanut Butter cereal, the eventual winner after a year-long search for a low-sugar and fiber-rich brand she actually enjoyed. Each spoonful would bring to her lips only one to two Puffins at most, the rest of them slipping back into the bowl during their shaky ascent. While she slogged through breakfast, I passed the time replying to any emails or texts that had landed in my inbox since yesterday morning.

Right on schedule, we had Carol in the bath. Many F-bombs later, we were finished. Next, just like always, she sat on the bed in a bathrobe while I stood in her closet and failed at several attempts to find a shirt she wanted to wear. Eventually she agreed to a blue sweater with a rolled neck, always one of her favorites.

As I helped her dress, I noticed that she was bleeding just above the knee. If, prior to her strokes, someone had told me what an obstacle a simple bloody knee could be, I never would have believed it. I'd seen it often enough by then to know that this would complicate the day pretty drastically. Various vascular issues left Carol prone to bruising. Simple bumps against a chair or a table or the edge of the bath could sometimes lead to an impossibly slow-healing wound. Some grew serious enough to require an emergency room visit. This wound, though, looked manageable. We started applying pressure, and after a half-hour, the bleeding slowed enough to where we could finish dressing and make it to the appointment on time.

I helped her into the wheelchair and guided her down the hallway to the elevator. In our building's parking garage, I lifted her into the car and folded the chair into the trunk. Then I drove us to the doctor's office, parked in the handicapped spot, lifted her back out of the car, and then wheeled her into the appointment. Like always, the process took over twenty minutes. Even so, we arrived two minutes early for our 10 A.M. session and were told that the nurse would come for us shortly.

The more time Carol and I spent together, pushed along by my growing acceptance of myself, Carol, and my circumstances, the more I reflected on how much of a strain my personality had put on our marriage in the years past. I sincerely believed that by trying to help her, I was fixing her, but she was never the one who needed fixing.

When we were younger, I feared that if Carol didn't get a little exercise once in a while, she would end up like her mother, who was in rough physical shape for most of her adult life. In my tendency to try to fix things before they were even broken, I urged my wife to join the YMCA, or some other fitness club. Sometimes she humored me and attended a yoga session or an aerobics class, but those efforts always faded.

Then, one day, she seemingly took my advice to heart. Our three sons had moved out, so we downsized to a smaller home and soon started to feel a little cooped up.

"Maybe it would be good to get out and take walks every day," I suggested.

Carol agreed, and went for a walk into Sewickley Village, a mile from where we lived at the time. The next day, she went out again. This became a full week of walking every day. My second-floor office looked out over the driveway, and I would see her depart every day around 10 A.M. Two hours later, I would see those little legs chugging back toward the house. Even at her typically pokey walking pace, I figured she'd walked a good six miles. I praised her on a regular basis for taking the bull by the horns. She would smile and go about her business.

This continued for several years. I probably patted myself on the back a time or two, taking some small amount of credit for the change.

Until one day when I went for a jog into town about twenty minutes after Carol had left for her morning walk. When I came to the edge of the village, I spotted her, a giant soft drink in her hand, as she made a turn up the street toward her best friend Linda's house and went inside.

Confused and frustrated, I finished my run, took a shower, and waited for my wife to return. An hour later, she came up the driveway.

"So," I said knowingly. "How was your walk?"

"Oh, fine," she said. "Same as always."

I smirked and presented my evidence. Whether I had expected

her to twist about getting caught in a lie, I can't be sure. But she just shrugged it off. For years, I had thought that I'd changed her somehow, but every day, Carol had been walking to the local bagel shop and grabbing a Diet Coke before heading straight to Linda's to gab for an hour or so. As I write this now, I kick myself for being such a pain-in-the-ass husband. That walk to Linda's and back was still a two-mile jaunt, and I should have just been happy with it instead of needing to be right.

The nurse took us back to an exam room, patched up Carol's knee, and took an INR reading to check her Coumadin levels. Anytime she dealt with one of those long-lasting bleeds, I worried that the dosage had gotten out of control. If her blood became too thin, it could be deadly.

After a little tape and gauze and a good INR reading, we headed home for a quick lunch and the noon pills. We had about forty-five minutes to enjoy lunch before we would need to leave for the podiatrist appointment at one o'clock. I had hoped to have enough time to get Carol a little rest, and maybe even run out to Sam's Club to pick up the prescriptions, but both would have to wait. As we drove home, we went past our church, St. James, which reminded me to make sure we attended Mass again soon. It had been a few weeks since our last visit, and both of us always felt better when we made it there on the regular.

I threw together some sandwiches for us—tuna for me and cheese with French's yellow mustard for her. I ate mine standing up and checking my emails while she picked through hers. Even though she didn't eat the crusts of her sandwiches, it still took my wife a solid fifteen minutes to get through an average-sized sandwich and wash down her pills.

As I put the lunch items away in our fridge full of food, I recalled how we'd always butted heads about the way Carol grocery shopped. In our little town, there used to be three grocery markets: a chain, a medium-sized independent, and a small corner store. Carol shopped at the smallest of them. And when she went, she would always pick up only the essentials: enough eggs for a few mornings, the fixings for a couple sandwiches, and a six-pack of Diet Coke. When that store closed, she promptly gave her business to the remaining independent store, never changing her habits.

This was fine, except that the bare shelves at home always bothered me, so I would nag her about at least getting some dinner supplies from time to time. When Carol was in charge of the shopping, the contents of our fridge always made it seem like we were moving out. Whenever the shopping fell to me, I would do exactly the opposite, as I loved buying in bulk. My backups always had backups.

I often let her know that I thought there was a better way to shop, and in doing so was imposing my own need for order and the way things ought to be. I'd convinced myself that Carol needed to be explained how things worked. In reality, all I'd been doing was trying to satisfy my own ego's needs. She would always acknowledge me with a polite nod before casually going about her day. This frustrated me, as it reinforced my mistaken belief that I was in this marriage alone.

After I started taking care of all the shopping post strokes, I learned that her shopping style had nothing to do with the purchase of food. When she went to the stores, she would listen to the cashiers' stories or problems, and they would always love her for it. That was also part of why she always shopped so small—she liked going more frequently because it gave her a chance to be out with her friends in the community. That was the Carol I'd come to eventually know, quietly going about life in her own way and without fanfare. After ten minutes of post-lunch chair rest in front of the TV, we had to leave, but not before a trip to the bathroom and an ill-timed tinkering with the many orchids and other potted flowers she kept all around the house. As always, on the way out the door, I grabbed my brown bag of meds and records. I threw her dinner pills in as well, in case we decided to eat out. We nearly made it all the way to the elevator before she asked for her purse. I hustled back for it, and we were on our way.

We arrived at the podiatrist precisely on time, which put us in good shape schedule-wise, because they could always get us out of there in twenty minutes. This was a good thing in part because I hated being late, but also because this was Monday, and Monday was movie day, Carol's favorite. As long as we remained on schedule, we would be done with our daily routine in time for a 4:30 screening.

Nothing compared to Carol's love for movies. Between Jennifer and me, she would see every new release, often twice. Of course, part of that was because every time she went to the theater, she enjoyed the biggest Diet Coke and largest box of popcorn she could get her hands on. My side of the bargain was that, from the moment we left the house until the moment we exited the theater, I would get to enjoy the perpetual little smile of excitement on Carol's face.

She needed those trips, and I needed them too.

We were called back to see the doctor almost immediately. As always, I held her hand while they clipped her nails, since she feared the sharp instrument the podiatrist used. By 1:40, we were hitting the road for the rehab facility and her two o'clock therapy appointment. I knew this trip would perk her up. She would be over the moon to see Wendy, Keirnan, and Debbie, to give everyone a virtual standup act, and to do exactly half of her exercises—no more, no less.

This trip didn't disappoint. It started with a few physical activities, then shifted to some mental exercises to stimulate her brain.

"Okay, Peanut," Debbie said, using the nickname she'd given Carol. "I'll ask you a question and you give me a list."

"Gotcha," Carol replied.

"Try not to overthink it. Just tell me the first things that come to mind."

Carol nodded, and Debbie looked down at the sheet on the clipboard she held.

"What are five things that you use only once?"

Before I could come up with an answer in my own mind, Carol had her first response ready.

"A rubber?"

I laughed so hard I fell into a fit of coughing.

After Debbie gathered herself, she pushed the list away. Carol had shut the test down in two words. But that was Carol—always clever. It's just that before the strokes, she had never really shared these kinds of thoughts with the world. Or maybe she'd just never shared them with me. To this day, her friends tell me that Carol was one of the funniest people around when they were younger. It's a mystery to me how I didn't know that. Perhaps it was me who'd had to open his eyes.

Although she hadn't gone to college, Carol was always one of smartest people I knew. Before her strokes, she was a voracious reader. I can't remember a time when she didn't have a book in her hand. She must have read three books a week. Sometimes she would go for the lighter reads, like James Patterson, but most times, she would be holding something in the John Irving category. She also loved television shows about medicine, whether a drama series or something more educational.

When we were younger, I often mentioned to Carol that she

should go back to school for nursing, since she liked to learn about these things and could manage the heavy reading load. She always politely passed on the notion. But that was never enough for me, so in the leadup to every new fall semester at the local colleges, I would ask again. Every time, she would oppose the idea with trademark silence. It was these instances where I'd start feeling underappreciated for my well-intended efforts. In retrospect, that was just my hungry ego finding a clever way to make an issue out of nothing and otherwise convince me that I was doing right by Carol. That's the Catch-22 about self-involvement, you are too involved with yourself to see the problem.

From the rehab facility, we had just enough time to make the movie. I knew I would need every minute of it, since the balancing act of buying the tickets and the concessions, and then getting situated in our seats always proved to be tricky. To complicate the matter, we were catching a movie at the theater she frequented with Jennifer, and I wasn't as used to it.

The refreshment stand sat in the center of the lobby, with the cashiers right next to the ticket taker. Usually, I took Carol to our seats and came back to get the food, but this was a movie I had been eager to see, so I didn't want to miss the start. With Carol locked in my arm, I began the tightrope walk of collecting two drinks and a popcorn while watching out for her safety. We stepped up to the self-serve soda station, and I grabbed a couple of smaller cups. "I want a bigger one," Carol said politely at a volume I could barely hear.

She had been such a trooper all day, so I grabbed the medium— which of course is an extra-large anywhere other than in a movie theater—and filled it with ice to minimize the fluids. Next, we stepped up to the popcorn counter, where I pointed to the second smallest size, plenty for an afternoon snack.

"We'll take the small bag there," I told the clerk.

"I want that one," Carol muttered, pointing.

I looked over at the popcorn receptacle lineup to note that the container she wanted was almost as large as her torso, let alone her stomach. This made me figure that the matter was negotiable.

"How about the middle one there?" I said.

"I want the big box," Carol announced, loud and clear.

The popcorn clerk leaned in and smiled. "You know, she always *does* get the big box."

I gave him a sidelong look. He wasn't helping.

"We still have dinner—"

"I want the fucking box," Carol hollered. It was the loudest I'd ever heard her speak in a year, and it caught the attention of everyone standing within thirty feet of us.

The clerk looked like he was stifling a laugh.

"You heard the lady," I said with a shrug. "Give her the fucking box."

"I guess she told you," the clerk replied as he started filling the fucking box.

I joined him in a belly laugh.

"It was kind of cute, huh?" Carol quipped.

The clerk held his smile for as long as it took him to fill the practically oil-drum-sized container. Somehow I managed to balance that gigantic tub, the two drinks, and my wife while grabbing my wallet as we worked our way over to the cashier.

We settled into our seats, and out came the afternoon pills.

About halfway through the movie, I noticed that Carol had somehow managed to dispose of half the giant box of popcorn. So I waited for her attention to be drawn and covertly slid the box under my seat. Later, with maybe fifteen minutes left in the film, she announced that she had to use the restroom. This was no surprise, as I'd gotten rather used to missing the climax of every movie. As we exited our seats, I was not surprised to hear my feet crunch through the massive pile of popcorn that had missed Carol's mouth. This had become such a common occurrence that the cleaning crew would always start with our mess first.

After we'd finished the long walk to the family restroom and completed her comb and lipstick routine at the sink, there didn't seem much point in returning just in time to see the credits roll. So we headed to the car.

We stopped at a favorite chain restaurant on the way home, a place where we always loved sitting at the bar. Once we had our seats, I pulled out her evening pills, and she shot me a dirty look. She hated having to take her pills in public.

"I'll have a Diet Coke please," she said to the smiling bartender.

I put my hand up. "Cancel that."

Carol furrowed her brow, looking ready to repeat her popcorn-tub performance, but I chased the expression away with a soft gaze. Due to Carol's blood-thinner, we had to limit her alcohol intake, so the routine had been to avoid any alcohol until 8 P.M., and even then, she could only have one or maybe two glasses of wine. But it had been a great day, so I figured it would be good to celebrate with an earlier drink.

"How about one of your big glasses of Chardonnay instead?" I asked. "With ice on the side, of course."

The bartender looked for confirmation from Carol, who had straightened up in approval.

"I'd love that." She beamed, and that smile hung on her face as we placed our standard order: a chicken Romano salad for the both of us.

We pulled back into the garage a few minutes before 8 P.M. I got Carol up to the condo and settled her into her chair with a rerun of *Frasier*. Then, I went to prepare a nightcap for the both of us. An Irish whiskey for me and a diluted Chardonnay for her. She barely even noticed me making us drinks. It never took more than a minute of that wonderful show to get her chuckling.

Though they were miles and miles away, I could easily picture our three boys sitting at her feet on the rug watching TV with us as we'd done so many times before. When they were young, we would gather around during Christmastime with mugs of hot chocolate and watch all their favorites: *Rudolph the Red Nosed Reindeer*, *Frosty the Snowman*, *Emmet Otter's Jug Band Christmas*, and *Charlie Brown*. As they got older, we traded the mugs for glasses of wine and the cartoons for *National Lampoon's Christmas Vacation*, but Carol and I would always look forward to the holiday season.

I caught her attention long enough to hand her that coveted white wine, and she blinked at me with breathtaking tenderness before looking back to the television. In those few blinks of the eye, an incredible shift in my thinking occurred. I'd let my relative inflexibility infiltrate our relationship too deeply for too long.

All those years, I had thought that by trying to fix Carol, I was loving her—that, in my tinkering with her life, I had been looking out for her best interests and otherwise taking care of her. Being a fixer, a neat freak, and expecting her to live my way must have made me tough to be with at times, but she had put up with me every day. During that time, I had failed to consider how that would have felt for Carol. She likely felt suffocated by my personality. For decades, I'd been squeezing my precious little bird too tight.

But all these things Carol did, she did out of deference, or affability, or maybe just to accommodate my more hardline views about how we should live. Did I have legitimate marital gripes along the way? Of course. We all do. But underlying my behavior for a lot of those years was a fundamental failure to appreciate my loyal and caring wife.

My thinking suddenly became clear: Carol was my little bird with a broken wing, and the only way to bring her back to health was to cradle her gently, always show kindness, and let her breathe and experience the world as she healed. The time for trying to change my wife had ended. I had squandered too many years on failing to show her the compassion she deserved, and to just let Carol be Carol. In this new phase of our relationship, I would do everything in my power to right that wrong.

Her contagious laughter punctuated the thought, and suddenly I felt lighter than I had in years. In my relaxed state, I noticed that my own laughter sounded heartier than usual. We watched a couple more episodes before my eyes grew heavy.

"Are you awake?" Carol asked me.

When I startled, I had a sudden sense that this was about the tenth time she'd had to ask me before I finally broke from my slumber. Falling asleep in my chair while watching TV at night had become something of a habit, and Carol woke me up the same way every time.

"I am now," I replied groggily.

"I'm ready for bed."

She had turned the TV off. I shook off the sleepiness and helped her to the bedroom, where we changed her into her pajamas and tucked her in. I gave her the teddy bear Matthew had gifted her at the hospital, hit the lights, and slid in next to her. Like every night, I found her free hand and squeezed tight.

"I love my Carol," I whispered.

"I love my Pogey," she whispered back.

Sleep wouldn't come. Carol was breathing heavily and would soon start to snore. My gaze found the big, red, digital numbers on the ceiling: 11:11 P.M. There would be just a moment of complete stillness in my mind before the anxiety about tomorrow would begin to pour in. On this night, I took immense pleasure in the rare lack of mental chatter.

Inspiration move me brightly,
light the song with sense and color.

– Robert Hunter
Terrapin Station

CHAPTER SEVEN
whether tragedy or turkey

It had been four years since Carol's strokes. One thing Dr. Tayal never told me was how quick-witted, comically irreverent, and observant my wife would become. Though her humor had been stunning since then, she'd also shown a tenacity beyond anything I could have ever imagined. At first, I attributed her changed personality to some sort of neurological loss of a mental filter, which would have explained her nearly immediate transition from a mild-mannered mother of three into a sparkplug of a woman with the vernacular and doggedness of a drunken sailor.

But then, after I'd had a little more time to observe how she handled her disability, I began to wonder if maybe I was in fact seeing the original Carol, the one who had always wanted to express herself this way. A particularly comic moment in our past came to mind, which supported that theory.

One winter in our home in Hilton Head, I was traveling to Kansas City for work almost weekly. I would pack my clothes every Sunday morning before leaving for the airport. Then, one Sunday, I discovered that one of the legs on a pair of pants I needed was badly wrinkled. Of course, this irked my meticulous nature.

"Is it really that hard to find the time to iron our clothes?" I groused.

As usual, she didn't reply.

"I don't ask much," I calmly argued, "but could you please make sure my travel clothes are ironed each week?"

She said she would, but then the same thing happened as I was preparing for my weekly trip the next Sunday. And then again the next. Every Thursday night, I would return home from Kansas City for a few nice days with my wife, but then every Sunday morning, I would find one pair of half-pressed pants as I packed for my Sunday evening flight.

Finally, I'd gotten myself worked into a bit of a mood about it, and trudged down the stairs to find Carol casually reading the newspaper

Photo: Singing Take Me Out to the Ball Game with her father Steward Perry.

81

in the dining room.

"I'm at a total loss," I said, with a smidge of scold in my voice. "Can you explain to me how this keeps happening?"

She snapped a dirty look at me, got up, and stalked off to the kitchen. I was so surprised by her uncharacteristically curt departure that I didn't follow her. But through the doorway, I could see her rummaging around in her purse. Finally, she found what she wanted and stormed back into the room.

"Listen, asshole," she said, "if you have a problem with these pants, go see the source!" With that, she slapped a piece of paper onto the counter.

My eyes wide, I leaned in to examine the paper. It was a dry-cleaning ticket. All that time, my clever wife had been hauling my clothes to the cleaners while I was away, and then taking credit for the ironing when I returned. She would just wheel them over to the cleaners on Monday morning, then pick them up on Thursday, remove the tags and any other evidence, and hang them in the closet. So that was the last time I complained about the pants, but we did find a better dry-cleaner.

My wife's infectious positivity permeated every facet of her life, but perhaps it shined brightest at the rehab facility. She had become a minor celebrity in that place, having been a patient there for five years. Everyone knew that when she walked in the door, they would be both entertained and moved. Their amusement would come from her inevitable cheating on her exercises, where Carol would routinely skip from her fourth rep to her fifteenth in any set of twenty. Or how she would drop a dozen F-bombs as she performed a therapy drill she didn't like. Though she hated the work, Carol never wanted to miss a visit. She never explicitly said it, but it was clear that she counted all those wonderful folks among her friends.

And they were moved by the same thing we all were: her one-of-a-kind, inspiring fortitude. One of the last times we visited that place was a few months before Carol's final hospitalization. She had been getting weaker for no apparent reason. We didn't know it at the time, but her heart was rapidly failing. As we entered the lobby area in the physical therapy room, the faces of the staff lit up, as they usually did upon her arrival. Carol saved her biggest smile for Wendy, one of her two main therapists. We hadn't been in for a session in almost two years, so Wendy was eager to give Carol a big hug.

"What's happened in the last two years?" she asked.

"Nothing much," Carol replied, blasé as ever.

Wendy glanced at me, and I rolled my eyes.

"How are you feeling?" Wendy asked, playing it straight.

All the gazes in the room found their way to Carol as we awaited her response.

"I'm fine."

The giggles kicked up all around us.

"Well," Wendy said as she took Carol's hand, "when I spoke to George earlier, he told me that since the last time we saw you, you broke a hip and got three pins, broke your shoulder, and had a heart attack, along with triple bypass surgery."

Carol gave a shoulder shrug, her message clear: *Nothing has gotten me down yet, so what's the big deal?*

Baffled as I'd always been about my wife's ability to let these various medical setbacks just roll right past her, I found that it was making perfect sense to me. She had always responded this way—to anything and everything—so why, when she'd come so close to death, should it be any different now?

––––––––––

2009. Early in November. Carol and I had just settled into our routine in Hilton Head, having arrived a week or so earlier. I'll never forget the call. We had returned with takeout from our favorite little Greek restaurant. I was arranging the plates as she took the boxes out of the bag. Whenever the phone rang, Carol would usually leap to pick it up, hopeful as she was that one of the boys would be calling. But this time, I was closer, so I picked it up.

"Hey, Dad," came the familiar voice. It was Chad. "I'm with the McCarthys, and it's not good."

My son sounded near tears. Carol must have seen the change in my expression, as she went for the other landline.

"Okay, you have both of us," she said.

"I'm at AGH," Chad explained. "Janet's not going to make it. She has some rare disease called Creutzfeldt-Jacobs. She might only live a month or so, at best."

It sounded to me like neither Chad nor his mother wanted to stay on the line a second longer, so I suggested that we hang up for now. By the time we got back in the same room, and I had taken her into my arms, Carol had lost her composure. I could picture Chad doing the same, some 700 miles away.

We had heard that Janet was seeing doctors, but the working theory had been that she was suffering from a vitamin deficiency, not a universally fatal brain disorder, so the news came as an overwhelming shock. For over fifty years, Janet and Carol, along with their friend Linda, had been the dearest of friends. We'd raised our kids together, attended their sporting events together, and enjoyed many dinners at each other's homes over the years. And just two months prior, at our fortieth wedding anniversary celebration, Janet had been the life of the party.

She and Carol were so close that the former would call the latter every morning at the same time, just to talk. Most of the time, the phone would hardly even be off the hook before Carol would start giggling. That was Janet, always able to make my wife laugh at will. And if I'd had anything I needed to say to Carol after that call came in every morning, I might as well have forgotten it, because nothing short of a three-alarm fire could ever hope to interrupt them. It was a perfect relationship; Janet got to be her silly and hysterically funny self, while Carol enjoyed a beautiful friendship, laughing the whole way through.

I suppose I should have sensed that something was amiss, since Janet hadn't called for the past few days.

As Carol's sobbing subsided, I promised her that we would immediately book flights back to Pittsburgh to say goodbye and make our peace. It was a good thing we did, as Janet would be gone less than two weeks later, at the age of sixty-two.

Carol had endured a ridiculously unfair, lifelong run of tragic deaths among her closest friends and family. It started with the untimely demise of two friends when Carol was still in high school. Then, from the late 1980s through the mid-1990s, the sheer number of dear friends and family members that my wife lost would have wrecked most people.

Carol lost her dear friend Polly Phillips, in 1993, from breast cancer at the age of forty-three. Despite her early death, Polly's memory remained strong in our lives.

"Do you remember that weekend with Polly and John?" I could ask Carol, and she would burst into laughter despite the pain of loss that accompanied the memory.

Polly Phillips may have brought Carol and me one of our favorite weekends ever. Sometime in the early 1980s, we had fallen in love with Cape Cod, particularly the small island of Martha's Vineyard. We had vacationed there for several summers with our boys, and had tried to get away there for long weekends as often as we could.

One September, Polly and her husband John joined us for a quick trip. Like Janet, Polly Phillips never took life too seriously and had an infectious laugh that would bowl you over.

We arrived at the rented cottage just as the sun had started to set. The four of us had barely brought in the first load of luggage and groceries from the rental car when John went on a mad search for towels and blankets. Not but a minute later, he reappeared and whispered in Polly's ear. She dropped her bag and grabbed his hand.

"I hate to do this," he said. "But my wife and I must take our leave."

"What the hell are you talking about?" I asked.

They looked at each other, and Carol knowingly giggled.

"If you must know," John announced coyly. "I've never done it on the beach before."

I chuckled through my disbelief. "Well don't let me stop you!"

Quickly they took their leave, scurrying over the deck and out into the fading light. It wasn't long before they returned through the sliding door, because Carol and I were still putting the last of the items into the fridge.

"That was fast," my wife quipped.

"I couldn't do it," John said.

A moment of awkward silence followed.

"Not that," he protested. "The minute we laid down, I couldn't stop hearing that damn Jaws song. *Dun-dunh...dun-dunh...dun-dunh.*"

We almost lost our balance from the laughter. John tore open a bottle of wine, and into the night, stories were told.

Carol's own smile and laugh were like a big candle in the room. I had watched so many people over the years set a spark to it and then soak in its joyous and extraordinary light. For the next four days and three nights, Polly and John had kept that flame lit. Every day and on into the night, we laughed until it hurt. We would lose Polly soon after, but those memories never faded.

About a year later, Mareena, her close friend and partner in the Perfect Presents business lost her life to domestic violence. Carol had

85

a knack for befriending good-hearted, caring, and giving people, and Mareena was one of those folks. My wife had jumped at the opportunity to spend large swaths of time with one of her closest friends, and the one occasion when I stopped by their office unannounced showed me the sort of time they were having.

They had been putting together a retirement gift for a post office worker, and Carol had pulled it all together in an incredibly creative way: a bronze mailbox to hold the gifts which doubled as a useful container, a box of chocolates that looked like stamps, and a small American flag, among many other clever goodies. She was so proud of it and her shop. Mareena had a way of highlighting some of my wife's best attributes—creativity, thoughtfulness, and making people happy.

Next, she would lose her favorite aunt, and Stew's sister, Carolyn. Between that trio, I'm not sure you could put together a warmer set of people. When Carolyn visited from Columbus, the three of them would get together and gab and grin about life until the moment she left. I remember one long-weekend visit, they'd decided to go on a walk, so I went about my elaborate day of yard work. Every time I saw them come around the block, they'd be laughing, and Carol would give me a cute wave and a smile. Carol just wanted to enjoy life, and her aunt always brought that spark to make to it happen. In 1995, while visiting Carol's sister, Lyn Anzalone, in San Diego, Carolyn suffered a massive brain aneurysm while sitting next to Carol.

At that time, we'd been living in the same house for over a decade, and Carol had developed a very close relationship with one of our neighbors, Kathy Gratton. Early in the summer of 1996, I joined Kathy and Carol at our recently purchased home in Hilton Head and got to see first-hand their wonderful connection, which was based on listening to each other, sharing their love of family, and laughing until their faces hurt. A few weeks later, while in the Charlotte (North Carolina) Airport, we received news that Kathy had suddenly passed. Carol, after four years of heartbreak, broke down into terrible tears that made my own heart break.

It always amazed me how Carol could find her way back after losing one great friend after another. She would cry her eyes out with each loss, and I would often find her looking through old pictures of the departed. But she would never succumb to self-pity or dwell on the unfairness of it all. Though I never asked her the question directly, my sense was that Carol had learned to live life in the moment, even long before that ethos became a cultural phenomenon. More than anyone I've ever known, she could cherish the memories in a way that kept those people alive in her heart.

I never really understood the true depth of my wife's personality—and perhaps the source of her sense of humor—until I had the occasion to live with Stew. Carol's father was like a Jimmy Stewart character: kind, gentle, compassionate, and principled—and after five years of living with him, it became clear how completely he had passed those qualities on to his daughter.

After Carol's strokes, when we moved to the new single story home, I had the place remodeled so the living room would be right in the middle of everything, making it easier for Carol and Stew to get to the spots where they could be the most comfortable. I installed a big television and new, plush sofas, the biggest sofa facing the front door and the gated stairwell at the opposite end of the open floor plan. From there, one could see just about everything and everyone in the main living space. Plus, this layout would allow me to pass Carol's favorite spot at least twenty-five times a day. This made it easier to ensure that she always had everything she needed.

Every morning, after we'd gotten her ready for the day, Carol would sit on that couch. Stew would join her a few minutes later, after he'd read the morning paper, and would sit at the opposite end. Some days, the schedule would be empty, leaving the two of them to sit side-by-side all day long. On the days with more activities, I would always make sure to return Carol to her favorite spot beside her father. Eventually, Stew would move out to San Diego to live with Lyn, but the few wonderful years he and Carol had together were spent smiling at each other from one end of the couch to the other.

Around five o'clock, I would make my way to the kitchen to start dinner for the three of us, but would first stop at the big entryway to the living room to check in on dinner plans.

"What are you in the mood for tonight?"

"Doesn't matter to me," Carol always replied.

"Whatever the chef wants," Stew would say.

"Neither of you have a preference?"

Two simultaneous shoulder shrugs.

For nearly five years, if we stayed in for dinner, this was the way it would go down. Then, one night, I pressed the issue, figuring that giving them some more specific options might help them contribute a decision.

"We have chicken breasts," I said. "And I think we have a few premade crab-cakes, plus some of that chili I froze last week."

"They all sound tasty to me," Stew answered, turning to his daughter. "What sounds good to you?"

"Doesn't matter to me," Carol said.

I threw my arms up in the air, grabbed some ground turkey breast and an orange vodka, and went out to the grill. From the patio, as I performed my usual overcooking of the turkey, I watched them sitting on the couch. They could sit there all day without saying a word to each other. Whenever a decision came up, they would always defer to the other. If I changed plans, no problem. If I changed them back, still no problem.

It wasn't until that moment on the patio that it truly struck me. Suddenly, Carol's behind-the-scenes and acquiescent disposition all made sense. It had been inescapable—like father, like daughter. Whether by genetics or learned behavior, they had become the two most easygoing people in the world.

They also shared an unparalleled level of humility. Nothing in their life was ever about them. Though Stew boasted of nothing, we all knew that his proudest accomplishment was the work he'd done to open the Brentwood Community Food Bank in the basement of his church. But that was Stew. His joy revolved around selflessly giving. This made him deferential to others in every decision, and gracious about everything good that ever happened to him.

But as I emptied that orange vodka, and as the turkey burgers continued their race past well done, something deeper occurred to me: Carol had also inherited her father's unyielding optimism. The old saying goes, "There's a silver lining in every cloud." I suspect that most people are like me, in that those clouds can quickly get thick enough to where they lose sight of any sign of silver streaks. Carol, though, could find them in a tornado.

That thought carried me back into the house with a smile on my face and three extra-crispy turkey burgers on the serving dish. Stew had worked his way over to Carol on his walker and was helping her get to her feet so she could stand at her own walker. Ever the gentleman, he let her lead the way into the kitchen. As they took their seats, I examined those charred discs of turkey and decided that I'd eliminated any chance they would still bear flavor.

Even so, I couldn't help but ask. "So, what's the verdict?"

"So tasty," Stew eagerly replied. "Thank you, George, for your fine work."

"Very good," Carol echoed.

I didn't learn this until much later, but Stew would wait until I exited the room to start delivering one-liners, along with the occasional eye-roll, about my subpar grilling skills. Apparently, he would get Carol, and sometimes my son Chad, into a good chuckle.

Whether tragedy or turkey, Carol always kept an even keel. The tragedy side required toughness beyond anything I could ever hope to display in my own life, and the patience it must have taken to endure my burned turkey called for a level of understanding that I've never been able to absorb, no matter how I try. Carol put it best one night before one of her many late-in-life surgeries. I asked her how she always found the will to overcome her health issues.

"Nothing gets me down," she said, offering that signature shrug.

Though I didn't realize it happening at first, I did manage to learn some measure of that resilience. Before Carol's strokes, I wouldn't have been the kind of man who could get up at odd hours of the night without complaint. Even those times when I did get grouchy, Carol's effect on me squashed those feelings in a hurry. Her spirit for life kept my chin up when things didn't go our way. How could I possibly be negative about such small matters in the face of this beaming light of positivity I called my wife? Even when I learned that my cancer had reached the point of incurability, and I was facing my own mortality for the first time, I knew exactly how to react. The answer was sitting right next to me.

That was the unfiltered Carol in a nutshell. Perhaps some strand of brain cells had been altered during those strokes, and the effect was to encourage a higher level of assertiveness. Or maybe she'd realized that there was nothing left to lose from being herself. Either way, she'd stepped out from her demure and unassuming persona and wandered into the limelight. Even more impressively, she carried on with the same carefree nature that had always endeared the world to her. She was now dependent on many other people to keep her healthy, and yet she was living life on her terms and making everyone laugh and feel inspired along the way.

CHAPTER EIGHT
feel the love

Courage is not having the strength to go on; it is
going on when you don't have the strength.
– President Theodore Roosevelt

One night in June of 2015, a social engagement put us on the road past the regular dinner hour. Since Carol's blood sugar numbers had been particularly wild of late, I decided to swing by a drive-through for a quick meal that might help us hedge against returning home to a low-blood-sugar situation. But when I handed Carol a chicken wrap and a fresh Diet Coke, she did something she had never done since her first stroke: she ignored them.

"What's wrong?" I said.

She gave a wide-eyed glance. "I can't breathe."

The day before, on Dr. Tayal's recommendation, we'd had our first scheduled appointment with a cardiologist named Dr. Suad Ismail. During this appointment, we learned that the warning signs for a heart attack are typically quite different for women than for men.

"Women don't experience chest or shoulder pains," Dr. Ismail said. "For us, heart attacks present as something more like a change in how we typically feel. If you see something out of the ordinary, head for the hospital."

Now, as we idled in that fast food parking lot, the terrifying picture started to fall into place. Ever since the strokes, we could always count on Carol eating anything you put in front of her. She never passed up a Diet Coke. Coupled with the difficulty breathing, this suddenly looked like an emergency situation. I roared for the highway that would bear us into Pittsburgh.

The nurses at AGH immediately ushered Carol into an exam room, where they performed a few tests that confirmed that she had in fact suffered a heart attack. Whenever I think back on this moment, I'm struck by how different things would have been if we hadn't met Dr. Ismail when we did. If we hadn't stopped for chicken, we wouldn't

Photo: With son Chad at PNC Park

have had the warning sign, and Carol might have died in her sleep that night.

My wife looked frightened and tired as they admitted her for the night, but otherwise, she acted like herself. I called all the people I normally called in these situations: my kids, her father and sister in San Diego, Jennifer, her cousin Jodi Jaynes in Ohio, and Linda Hoehl. When I spoke with the boys, I assured them that their mother wasn't in any present danger. Chad insisted on coming back from Nashville to visit anyway, since he hadn't been home in a while. He and his then-fiancée Catherine had moved there to embark on new careers. Though it could have been under better circumstances, I knew that Carol would be thrilled to see him.

Next, I left a message for Dr. George Magovern, Jr., the only heart surgeon I knew, and also one of the top cardio-thoracic surgeons in the country. I knew that heart attacks sometimes repeated themselves, so I figured if I could get Dr. Magovern involved, Carol would be in good hands.

The next morning, I picked Chad up at the airport.

"How's Mom?" he asked the moment he slid into the car.

"You know the answer to that."

"She's fine."

We had a good laugh.

"Are we worried?" Chad asked.

"Just tests right now. No further heart attacks, so that's good."

The moment we came through the door to Carol's room at AGH, the proud mother's eyes grew wide. I'd kept the visit a surprise, so the reunion was a bubbly one. Linda visited later that morning, as did another good friend, Mary Jane Platt. Jennifer stopped in around lunch, as well. They all brought laughter and stories, while Carol told everyone she was doing just fine.

That afternoon, after the nurses wheeled Carol off for further testing, Chad and I retreated to the cafeteria. We caught up on life, Nashville, and his thoughts about where he and Catherine might live after the wedding. I missed them terribly and prayed every day that they would return to Pittsburgh.

Back from the cafeteria, we found Carol's room empty. A nurse stopped in and told us she would escort us to the interventional cardiologist's office. He had loaded the films from the scans of Carol's heart onto his computer, and he had some thoughts on how we might proceed. The doctor had turned the large monitor on his desk so it faced the two chairs set up for guests. The image on the screen looked like black and white abstract art. Our host demonstrated an excellent demeanor as he explained all the preliminaries in a way I could understand. The gist was that they had run the tests so they could assess the level of Carol's blood flow near her heart.

"So, how does it look?" I asked.

"May I be frank?"

I nodded, as a tight knot formed in my stomach.

"I don't know how she's alive right now," he said, his eyes kind but intense. He pointed to a spot on the image. "This little aortic area is known as the widow-maker. It's more than ninety-five percent blocked. What that means is that Carol is hanging from the edge of a cliff by her fingers. And that's not even considering the mitral valve issue."

The knot leapt from my throat to my eyes, where it presented in the form of tears.

"She's on her way to the cardiac ICU right now," the doctor added gently. "I don't want to take any chances."

"Surely, something can be done," I said.

"There's three ways you deal with this. First, a stent. But if I tried that, it would likely cause her whole arterial system to explode. So that's out."

A tear spilled over my cheek.

"Second, there's medication. But unfortunately, her disease is too far advanced for that option."

He took a long pause. "Ordinarily, surgery would be an option, but the cardiology report says that her left ventricle isn't pumping strong enough to withstand it."

The harsh reality robbed me of my ability to speak. And I knew I couldn't look over at Chad, or I would lose what remained of my composure.

"I don't have anything to tell you that you can put your hopes into," the doctor said. "If surgery isn't an option, then I'm afraid Carol's time will be very short."

The dam burst. I fell into a shoulder-lurching sob, the kind of cry that I didn't even know I had in me. I grabbed a couple tissues from the well-placed box on the desk and rejoined the conversation that my son had continued with the doctor.

"What do we do next?" Chad was asking.

"I'm not a surgeon," the doctor said, "so it's not my place to make that decision." He sighed and looked steadily at me. "But I'd get your affairs in order."

Chad and I left his office with all the grace of a couple of zombies. We stood in one of the hospital's many bright corridors, the bold light and the ad-barren walls making me feel anxious. The hospital wasn't allowing visitors to the cardiac ICU, so we returned to the cozier confines of the cafeteria. On the way down, since I couldn't bear repeating the situation to my other two sons, I asked Chad to call his brothers and get them to town.

By the evenings at AGH, the cafeteria always seemed to echo the day's activity. It was never as busy, and those in the room typically appeared either tired or reflective. In this quiet atmosphere, I attempted to process the news we'd just heard. I finished my first cup of coffee quickly, and was just getting back up for more when I ran into another cardiologist managing Carol's case. He told me that he had seen the films and agreed that not much could be done.

Dazed, I returned to my seat across from Chad. "Everybody seems to be counting her out," I said.

After a long and quiet second cup of coffee, we went to the fifth floor and found our way to the Cardiothoracic Specialty Care Unit. I saw Carol sleeping through the sliding glass door to her room. She had more leads coming from her body than I had ever seen before, and at least three large monitors set up around her beeped and whirred and blinked numbers in different colors. I choked back a fresh round of tears, pulled the door open, and rushed to the chair next to the bed. For the next several minutes, I watched those numbers blink. The whole room felt as critical as my wife's condition.

Soon after, her nurse Taylor entered for a checkup, and proceeded to explain every monitor and the meaning of every number they displayed. In a nutshell, it all boiled down to a constant calibration of Carol's blood pressure with a wide variety of medicines. I had always been a numbers person, so I asked for the normal ranges, and he related them to me.

About an hour later, Dr. Ismail stepped up to the sliding glass door with a concerned smile. She waved me to join her in the hall. I complied. Gracefully and honestly, she broke down the situation: it was a cardiac Catch-22. First, she confirmed that, without surgery, death was likely imminent. But for surgery to be possible, we would have to wean her off the blood thinner. Meanwhile, thicker blood presented a danger because of the widow-maker blockage. To make matters worse, the mitral valve was causing wild blood pressure fluctuations, which meant that Carol could quickly drop into heart failure or have another attack. Dr. Ismail wrapped up with a polite dodge of my questions about whether Carol could survive surgery, but assured me that they would do their best to keep her alive until then.

The knot jumped from my stomach and radiated across my chest.

I squeezed Carol's hand and fixated on the flashing numbers. It felt like I had to wait an eternity for every new update, even though the truth was that they happened precisely every minute. In those tense seconds waiting for them to refresh, the discussions about death repeated in my head. I wasn't ready to let Carol go. I wasn't ready to be alone. The thought of losing her made me think about what my life, her life, our lives had meant. Though I would end up asking myself the question a thousand times, that was the first moment it had formed in my brain: had I done enough for her?

For our whole life together, Carol had deferred to my preferences, and in so doing, had allowed me to reach higher with my career. But at some point, I had lost my way and started casting onto her the burdens of what I expected of marriage. And what did she do? She shouldered them. She soldiered on, always trying to please me and make things right. It wasn't that we had ever fallen out of love; it was that I had found ways to dodge humility or convince myself that the things I'd been doing were satisfying my half of the bargain.

In my mind, providing a steady income, a home, a faithful man, and a father to three sons had been enough. And if you were grading my obligations as a husband in the traditional sense, I'd have passed. But marriage didn't equate to love unless you gave it love. This was what I first truly discovered in those moments after the first stroke, and understood even more so after the second. With that knowledge, and for the five years since, my goal had been to do what I could to let her feel the love.

In pursuit of that objective, I'd traveled unwittingly along a journey of romance, experiencing it in a whole new manner, getting to know her in this wonderful new way. Carol, with her emboldened individualism, and me with my newfound openness, tolerance, and tenderness were what made it all possible. Like new lovers in their early twenties, we'd developed inside jokes, ways of being intimate, and even the normal tension that occurs as two become one. We'd travelled, laughed, sung songs to each other, and recited those three most important words more often than ever. Still, as I sat at her bedside—next to what I feared might be her deathbed—the question nagged at me. Had my efforts been enough?

Carol's quiet whisper broke me from my trance, but I couldn't quite make out what she said.

"Sorry, can you say that again?" I asked as I leaned in closer.

She tried to sit up a little straighter. "So..." she said, her lips softening into a clever smile. "How's everything going?"

Taken aback by the question, I cocked my head to one side.

After the strokes, the responsibility for starting and sustaining conversations fell almost exclusively to me. Sometimes Carol would engage, and sometimes, she wouldn't. I would always run out of things to say after a while, and we would wind up sitting in uncomfortable silence. During a long car ride earlier that year, I'd implored her to feel free to start conversations from time to time. In reply, she'd turned to me and said, "So...how's everything going?"

I'd had a good, long laugh in the car, and there I was having it again in that hospital room.

Chad returned, and we decided that the two of us would stay the night in the hospital. But as we began to situate our chairs and pillows, the nurse coming on for the night shift seemed like she was preparing to tell us to leave. Taylor talked to her for about a minute. Eventually, after quite a lot of nodding, the other nurse relented. My son and I settled in for the night.

Over the last couple hours, Carol's numbers had been trending in the wrong direction. The worry crept back into my mind. I kept picturing the image the doctor painted of my wife holding onto the edge of a cliff by her fingers. *Can she make it to surgery?* I wondered anxiously. *Can her weakened body sustain it? What will I do without my wife and best friend?*

Somewhere in the middle of my fretting, Dr. Magovern returned my call. It felt like a week since I'd left that message. After a brief exchange about how he'd be stuck out of town until Saturday night, he said something calming, if only slightly.

"I'm hearing the same thing you are," he said. "That she's not going to make it. But just remember, I haven't seen the films yet."

One of the top heart surgeons in the country had given me a sliver of hope. Now, we just needed to keep Carol alive until Dr. Magovern could get home.

The nurse stepped in and turned out the light, leaving us with the bright blue glow of the monitors. Between unwanted dozes, I would sit up and watch those flashing numbers and beeping sounds. These indicators would become something of an obsession for me for the next hundred hours. Any time the numbers fell out of range, the alarm bell sounded, and I worried that she might pass away, right there in front of me, at any moment. I would pop up from my chair in a desperate search for a nurse, even though I knew they were always quick to respond. Only after they had steadied the situation, and calm returned to the room, would I relax even a little.

Early the next morning, sunlight poured through the window, rousing me from my half-sleep. I sprang up reflexively, afraid that Carol had gotten up to go to the bathroom. To my relief, I found my wife and son snoring the morning away. I sat up in the chair and assessed Carol's numbers. So far, so good. Though I had been happy to wake to relative normalcy, the intensity of the surroundings concerned me. Even if Carol made it through, she might still have entered the downhill phase in her life. That familiar pang of pain returned to my stomach.

Chad soon stirred, and we went in search of coffee and breakfast. Around this time, Sean arrived from the airport and joined us. Carol lit up like a firework when she saw him trailing us through the door.

"Oh, there you are!" she said.

The way Carol's relationships with the boys flourished as they became adults was a joy for me to watch. Looking back now, I have to smile at how there was a time when she thought that because of sports she would never be as important to them as their father. Of course I had told her back then that they would grow closer as the boys grew older. To my great pride and delight, they proved me right and then some, particularly during the home stretch of their mother's life.

By this point, Sean was always reaching out and doting on Carol like never before. She clearly loved every second of it. Watching him greet and attend to her now reminded me of the Thanksgiving when I first noticed this tendency in him. For years, Carol had taken care of Thanksgiving dinner at our house. Her two specialties were her moist-yet-crispy stuffing, and a sweet potato casserole that was out of this world. At some point, Sean started to help her with these dishes. Then, after the strokes, when she'd become unable to prepare the food on her own, Sean reversed the roles and had Carol help him. They always laughed whenever she would drop a quarter of the ingredients on the floor. Every year, she would get so excited about Thanksgiving, and I knew that a huge part of the reason was her cooking time with Sean.

Sean stroked his mother's hair as he sat beside her hospital bed.

"I love it when you do that shit," Carol said.

Taylor had entered just in time to overhear. He erupted in laughter with the rest of us. "It's good to know she doesn't just talk like that with me," he said.

Later that day, my good friend Howard Cohen stopped by to see us. Howard practiced as a cardiologist and specialized in cardiovascular disease, so he wanted to see if he could help. Since we were still waiting for Dr. Magovern, and didn't know what his verdict would be, I figured it couldn't hurt to authorize my friend to look at Carol's records and X-rays.

We went out to the nurses' station, where Howard proceeded to draw a simplified version of what he would do if given the chance to perform such a procedure. Although I'll never fully understand the medical reasoning behind it, by Howard's own admission, his drawing represented an inventive strategy. The basic gist was that he would enter via an artery and use some sort of robot to sneak past the widow-maker blockage and create a bypass, which would then allow him the chance to work on the mitral valve.

I stepped away from the diagram for a minute and glanced in at Carol, who was one bad blood pressure swing from death. I considered Howard to be one of the most even-tempered and intelligent people I knew, and I still think that. So, if he was telling us that this would be our best solution, I was all for it. Howard promised to reach out to Dr. Magovern to discuss. For now, we would have to wait.

The next morning, as Sean, Chad, and I sat on the window side of Carol's bed, Matthew strode up to the sliding glass door. Carol followed our gazes and lit up. The trip from Montana to Pittsburgh required at least two flights that cost Matthew over a thousand dollars each time. He had started making the journey more frequently since his mother's strokes, but his presence still tended to coincide with downturns in Carol's health. This realization seemed to occur to my wife in the next moment, as she turned away from greeting Matthew and shot a glare at me.

"What's going on here?" she asked.

I remained silent.

By then, Matthew had come to the side of the bed. He had bought his mother another teddy bear.

She smiled wide as she pulled it close. Then, ever the direct one, she said, "Seriously, why are you here, Matthew?"

The way the question came out made us all laugh. The truth was that everyone involved believed that it wouldn't be good for Carol's heart to include her in the stress of every medical discussion. Since nothing concrete had been decided yet, I'd been okay with it, but I could see that the boys and I needed to figure out a way to deliver the stark truth. We exchanged some hangdog looks, none of us sure of what to say. Taylor returned to collect Carol for tests, so we were saved by the bell.

After the tests were over and Carol was back in her bed, my sons and I gathered around her bedside and explained that the doctors might need to perform a corrective surgery, but that we would wait for Dr. Magovern to give us his thoughts before proceeding with anything. Like she always did, Carol took the news in stride, and said very little. She was courageous that way, rarely ever showing her fear.

From that point forward, we camped out in that little room, breaking all the visiting hours rules related to time and number of guests. After a couple days we began to take shifts, but there was always at least one Shannon in the room in addition to Carol from 7 A.M. to 7 P.M. There were occasional bouts of laughter, and a few stories told, but mostly we concerned ourselves with being next to this woman who meant so much to all of us.

As the week wore on, I could see that something needed to be done. Carol's numbers trended further from normal, and the medical team's efforts to stabilize her took longer and longer. Every time they got her back into a safe zone, those vitals would immediately head in the other direction, causing another mini-crisis. The whole thing felt like a long volley in a tennis match, with nobody wanting to give up the point. Time had become the worthiest of adversaries.

At 9 P.M. that Saturday night, Dr. Magovern called me as he disembarked his plane from Chicago. We set a meeting for first thing the next morning. Chad and I arrived an hour early. As we sat in silence, I couldn't help but dwell on the cardiologist's opinion that

Carol wasn't suited for surgery, and on Howard's plan for how to overcome a supposedly insurmountable obstacle.

Dr. Magovern broke the spell of worry when he appeared in the hall and waved us out of Carol's room. I approached him with a mouthful of questions, and a pit of swirling doubt in my mind. He beat me to the punch by a mile.

"I've scheduled Carol tomorrow for a triple bypass at six in the morning."

I didn't know how to respond. I had to replay the words I'd heard, just to make sure I had them right. Eventually, I managed a half-coherent question about the condition of Carol's arteries. "The plaque?"

He explained in clear terms that it was a genetic condition that led to Carol's arteries being full of plaque, and that, yes, the existence of this plaque posed a high risk of triggering another stroke, especially since Carol would be off her Coumadin for surgery.

But then he said, "I took a long look at those films, and I think I found a tiny place I can clamp onto."

Meanwhile, I was willing to clamp onto any little hint of hope. I knew the procedure would be risky, but Dr. Magovern's confidence brought significant relief. I may have even smiled.

"Is she ready?" I asked.

"We don't have a choice," he replied. "If we don't do something soon, she won't make it."

The answer, though terrifying, didn't come as a surprise, as I'd been hearing it all week.

"Besides," he added. "I know I'm not going to sleep tonight. And you certainly aren't going to sleep. So, let's get on with it."

With that, he strode confidently from the room.

This was how the door on Carol's chances cracked open just enough to let in a slice of light. We had a plan in place. It was still a long shot, and despite our surgeon's renowned skill, I knew that there was a very distinct possibility that the door would slam shut in just a short twenty-four hours. First, we had to get her to tomorrow morning.

Sean and Matthew joined us a while later, and we spent the whole day as a family in Carol's little room. We took turns sitting in the seat at the head of the bed, holding Carol's hand and talking with her. Like most families, we had our complexities, but I felt overwhelmed with pride at the way we supported each other. We shared the news with

Carol, albeit with the breeziest possible spin we could give it. Then, with the dangerous surgery just hours away, we all had a few final words with her.

Sean led off with the pep-talk Carol needed. In the last handful of years, Sean had been much sillier with Carol, so the talk came from a place of humor. She giggled appreciatively. Then, he planted a peck on her forehead as he relinquished the chair to Chad.

"I know you'll be fine," Chad told her. "Because Catherine's going to need help picking out flowers for the wedding."

It was true. Carol would have to make it through this surgery because there was no way she would allow herself to miss that wedding. She had been thinking about that day for the whole year since we learned of the engagement. Chad kissed his mother on the forehead and gave up the chair to Matthew.

Before Matthew could sit, she reached out and grabbed his hand.

"I don't want to die," she said, loud and clear.

The boys and I all glanced at each other, acknowledging the rare expression of concern Carol had just shared. We didn't want that either.

My heart ached and warmed at the same time. I felt the fear that my wife was expressing but also experienced a wave of affection for their connection and the way Matthew responded. The two of them had spent a lot of time together back when I was traveling for work, and it gave me great joy to see them bonding again. He assured her that she would make it through, and after a few more minutes of this, he kissed her on the forehead and rose from the chair. The boys then left us to be alone.

Now it was my turn in the seat. Had I done enough to make her feel the love? With my wife's life in the balance, and with these being possibly our last moments together, the answer became a bit clearer. It was likely that I would never convince myself that I'd done enough, but I did feel like the luckiest guy in the world in that I'd had the chance to fall in love with this woman again. That wonderful revelation spurred, in all its unfettered glory, this all-consuming feeling of love. It buzzed through me, the beautiful noise of it drowning out any thought, opinion, or expectation I'd ever had.

In that moment of purest love, panic crystalized in the form of a question: *Is this really all the time I have left with her?* From Carol's bedside, just as I had so many times from the pew after Communion, I started making desperate offers. *What's it going to take? My life for hers?* No immediate answers came.

I sighed, and might even have gotten mad for a moment at the thought that we had no sooner fallen in love again than I risked losing this wonderful wife of mine. Fear came directly from love, because when you have something extraordinary, you don't want to lose a single bit of it. It didn't take me the better part of five decades to fall in love. It just took me a lifelong journey toward humility to fall all the way.

Carol tugged at my hand and repeated her fear of dying. Though I shared that same fear, I promised that we wouldn't let that happen to her. After a few minutes of encouragement, I just sat still with her, running my fingers through her hair and over her hand, trying to comfort her. At one point, I adjusted her caged-heart necklace, prompting a silent smile.

We had experienced so many bouts with silence in our later years. Sometimes, I would want nothing more than just to reach out and make a connection on something, a way for us both to feel the love. At some point along the way, I found a little bond that tied us together, and I would break these quiet moments with a tune—my take on a number I'd often heard Bing Crosby sing on the radio when I was a child.

"Over in Killarney…"

And despite the fear that this day might be her last, she responded to the call right on cue.

"…many years ago."

I squeezed her hand.

"Me mother sang a song to me…"

She squeezed back.

"…in tones, so sweet and low."

"Just a simple little ditty…"

I brushed her hair with my fingers.

"…in her good old Irish way."

She closed her eyes.

"For I'd give the world for her to sing…"

And we sang the last line together.

"…that song to me this day."

I leaned in and kissed her. Not long after, she was asleep and breathing softly. I took one last, long look at those heart numbers just before I left the room. For tonight, at least, my darling wife would be okay.

HAPPY BIRTHDAY
to my husband,
my soul mate,
my very best friend.
I love you.

Love Carol

– Carol Shannon
*Carol's message on the birthday card she gave me in
2014, 2015, and 2016. Out of the 5,000 greeting cards at Rite Aid,
she chose the same one three consecutive years without realizing it.*

CHAPTER NINE
it finds you

December 28, 2016

Carol's first surprise birthday party was New Year's Eve, 1987. In the eighteen years of our marriage up to that point, we'd lived in four states and moved five times. But we'd lived in that house on Thorn Street for four years, which was tied for our longest stretch yet. I had missed making a big deal over her fortieth, so I went full bore for her forty-first. At the time of that party, Sean was sixteen, Chad was thirteen, and Matthew was ten. They did a great job helping keep the sixty or so guests quiet as her friends Linda and Janet led Carol into the house.

The look on her face was one that I've never forgotten. Most of our family and all our friends at the time were there. The kids transformed the dining room's hardwood into a dance floor, and there, through a steady stream of Motown and oldies, Carol and I danced all night, a relatively new thing for us.

Much to the disappointment of my wife, I never danced until about a year before her surprise party. I'd secretly taken six weeks of Arthur Murray dance classes. When the first song came on at a big New Year's Eve party that year, I asked Carol to dance. She nearly fell over in shock, and once again when she got a gander at my new moves. We took to the dance floor and never left, letting it all hang out.

Her surprise party proved no different. For days after, Carol often mentioned that she couldn't believe how all these people had gathered just for her. She'd always been that way: so humbled and moved by the gestures of others.

Here we were again, nearly thirty years later, an hour before Carol's seventieth birthday party, and she had no idea the surprise in store for her. I peeked in on her and asked if she was excited to check out the new restaurant in town. She nodded and went back to putting on her lipstick. She looked beautiful in the new outfit I'd bought her for Christmas, a spiffy black and white number purchased just for this

Photo: Carol's seventieth surprise birthday party, her last.

occasion.

In some ways, I couldn't believe we had reached this milestone. She had started down the path of troubled health at the age of sixty-three, and back then, the odds of her making it to seventy seemed slim. The doctor had implied as much. When the second stroke hit, it seemed that these events might occur repeatedly, and each time, they would take a little piece of her life along with them. Her closest brush with death had come when she faced that nearly miraculous heart surgery. Post-bypass, her first words to Dr. Magovern were, "I'm fine."

Even though it all seemed so far away now, I couldn't help but smile at the memory of her one-year post-stroke follow-up with Dr. Tayal in May of 2011. I'd felt a sense of pride that day as my wife and I walked hand-in-hand from the parking garage down the long corridor to the hospital. She had come such a long way from boxing gloves and thickened liquids. She hadn't even needed a wheelchair or a walker to make the long trek.

When we stepped off the elevator in the medical office building, we stood face to face with Dr. Short, the same doctor who had predicted a swan song for Carol the year prior. His eyes bulged when he saw her. He shot a look at me and then back at her.

"Oh, I see you are still with us," he said.

You're still with us? I thought. *Anger boiled within me. Still unkind, still cold. Some things never change.* Then, I took a deep breath. *Humility, George.*

"We're doing just fine," I said, nicking my wife's favorite line.

As we glided down the hall, I muttered less than complimentary things about that doctor under my breath. Carol tried to tell me to be quiet, but she couldn't stop giggling.

My eldest son tapped his watch, his signal that we had to go. Sean had first suggested that we make it a big birthday bash, and I could see that he was excited about it. So was I. The surprise would go off without a hitch. We used the cover of the holiday season to explain why all three of our sons were in town.

Carol's birthday was on New Year's Eve, so we decided to pick an off night for the celebration, December 28th. Carol loved to go out to eat, and a local restauranteur, Robin Fernandez, had just opened a new place in town, Bruneaux, which provided the perfect pretense to get her out of the house none the wiser. Plus, some recently arriving visitors could help cover the story. Chad and Catherine had just returned from spending Christmas with Catherine's family in Scranton. That summer, the two of them were married in a lovely ceremony at a local nature center on a perfect blue-sky day. Carol had indeed gotten her chance to help Catherine pick out a wonderful array of flowers for the occasion, which served as a memorable backdrop for a day filled with laughter and nearly enough dancing to last a lifetime. Given how much Carol still loved chatting with her son and new daughter-in-law about the wedding, I knew they would provide compelling misdirection for the upcoming surprise.

As they settled in with Carol, Sean and I slipped out under the auspices of running to the wine store to get some special bottles for the occasion.

When we arrived at the restaurant, and I saw firsthand how many people were so incredibly fond of my wife, it felt like an electric charge was climbing up my spine. I couldn't wait to see that unforgettable look of joy on her face once more. I texted for the boys and Catherine to lead Carol down. Our friend Chris Wu started preparing his fiddle.

I chanced a look outside and spotted the wheelchair rolling toward the place—we had since moved back from the hills to a smaller condo just a block from downtown Sewickley. Carol couldn't walk very far on her own anymore, and as much as she'd always hated that wheelchair, we had managed to come to an agreement. She would allow us to push her around in it, so long as we promised to ditch the thing just before we entered any public places.

When they arrived, I stepped into the small vestibule and prepared to walk her into the building. As per our pact, Chad, Catherine, and Matthew stopped just short of the door to help Carol out of the chair.

You can see into the forward edge of the restaurant from inside the vestibule, so as Matthew and Chad helped Carol to me, she managed to catch a glimpse of the Hoehl family standing in front of the waiting crowd. It was apparently at this moment that she sniffed out the surprise, because the second I opened the door, she loudly posed a simple question:

"What the fuck is going on?"

The twenty people closest to the door went to pieces. In retrospect, I couldn't have imagined a better way for her to enter her seventieth birthday party.

When she saw the size of the crowd, she lit up in a way that made my wish come true and then some. Though I don't have video from the 1987 party, the reaction for her seventieth wins in a landslide. Linda and Greg's son Matt recorded the scene, and I have watched that video over and over in the days since. My favorite part is the way her giddy laughter turns into open-mouthed amazement the moment she sees the crowd. If dementia ever robs my memory bank, those five seconds will be among the last precious gems I'll hold onto.

As the calls of surprise subsided, Chris started up with a beautiful rendition of "Happy Birthday," and the crowd joined in. As the serenade concluded, Carol delivered her signature move, the left arm shoulder shrug punctuated by an upturned palm.

Our sons had prepared a few words, with Matthew beginning. A few seconds into his speech, Carol spotted someone special in the crowd, and cut in.

"Oh!" she exclaimed. "There's Wendy!"

Wendy replied with a cheerful wave. The crowd erupted with laughter. When it died down, Matthew concluded his speech.

"Mom," he said, "you have been my strength, and I love you."

"You better love me a lot," she fired back, sending the crowd into hysterics.

Chad noted in his remarks that when he was a child, his mother had given him the sage advice to be kind to everyone, and that the crowd that night was a perfect example of that wisdom. People from every era of Carol's life were there, from old friends to new. My sister Barb, having buried their youngest daughter just a couple months prior, had come with her entire heartbroken family. The Jaynes had made the trip from Columbus.

Sean finished up with a sentiment that had become true of the whole family. Whenever the boys came to see us, they would always give Carol a long, tight hug, to which she would always respond, "I love you, and don't you ever forget it." I'd heard her say it to each of them many times. And now here was Sean, returning the thought in kind.

"Everyone in this room loves you, and don't you ever forget it."

That was about as much standing as Carol could do in a stretch, so we sat down right in the middle of the restaurant at a table. It felt like a wedding, the way people kept coming over to see us. Every time I got up to mingle, I would glance back at the table, and there was always someone new there, talking with her, making her laugh and feel special.

My daughter-in-law Catherine had made a large poster centered by one of my all-time favorite photos of Carol, a silly yet somehow glamorous pose at a Saturday afternoon barbecue for the high school football team. In it, she has her head cocked to the side like a movie star, a slight smile, and a lit cigarette in her hand—a perfect snapshot of my wife's carefree attitude. Next to it, she left a big white space forpeople to sign. By the end of the night, warm words filled the space to capacity. There was just so much love in that room.

The next morning, I went for a long walk, taking one of Carol's favorite routes from those couple years when she'd feigned exercise while she was really visiting her friend Linda. I walked past an old swimming and tennis club. Carol took tennis lessons there one summer, and quickly proved to be one of the worst players in the history of the sport. She hated every minute of it, but had tried anyway, and in part because of my encouragement.

As I walked on, I couldn't help but be overwhelmed by the outpouring of support we had witnessed the night before. But it went beyond just a night—a whole community of assistance had been present from day one. Though I knew we had raised good kids, I never could've imagined how wonderful each of them would be with their mother. Matthew called all the time. Sean visited as often as he could. Chad would often take on my role as caregiver so I could get away for a few days.

My siblings, Jimmy and Lennie, visited frequently and made Carol feel special. Barb would come stay for a couple nights now and then, always providing us with some laughter and help. Tommy checked in on us often, his conversations with Carol always leaving her delightfully silly. Jodi and David would sneak away from their busy lives raising a family, whether the occasion for a visit was a good or a bad one.

My walk took me to one of the most beautiful spots in town, a street lined with trees that must be at least 150 years old. I thought about the generosity our friends had shown over the years, how they had opened their homes for visits, invited us to dinner, reached out to spend time with Carol, or stopped by with food, especially when we had just returned from a hospital visit. Their selflessness humbled me. The truth was that they had all played the role of caregiver in their own ways.

When I hit my turnaround point near Little Sewickley Creek, I knew there was one last place I needed to see: the location of Carol's first surprise party.

As I made the two-plus mile walk to our old house, I thought about how, a few months after Carol's second stroke, we'd started going back to church. Because of my wife's extensive morning routine, we had started going to Saturday five o'clock Mass rather than forcing the issue on Sundays. We would get Carol dressed up in her best clothes—which basically just meant dress pants instead of the usual athletic pants, and maybe a little extra jewelry. At communion, I would let a good portion of the congregants go ahead of us, because I didn't want to halt the procession with our slow pace. When we would finally reach the front, Father Dan would see us, smile, and come down the aisle to meet us.

To return to our seats, we passed the front of the altar, which meant that we also passed the additional sacrament of wine. It probably would have been better for her legs to get back to the pew quickly, but there was zero chance that Carol wouldn't stop for a sip of the good stuff. She always gave the appearance of wanting to do her duty as a good Catholic, but I knew she was sneaking an extra nip.

We would be met with warm smiles and kind faces during our slow walk back. Back at our seats, I would have just enough time to kneel and ask God for more days for Carol. Since that blunt doctor had sent me into impromptu prayer in the darkened alcove, my wife had lived six-and-a-half years beyond the strokes. In this way, it had become a daily renegotiation, and I would take any time I could get.

Our Saturday night routine became taking our good feelings from Mass to our favorite dinner destination. We kept a 7 P.M. reservation, allowing for just enough time to belly up at the bar for a pre-dinner drink. Every time we pulled into the roundabout of the restaurant, Ron, the head valet, would help me perform a perfectly choreographed routine to ensure Carol's swift passage from the car to a cozy glass of Chardonnay.

The large set of windows at the head of the restaurant afforded Lynn, the regular Saturday night bartender, the chance to see us coming. While Ron and I helped Carol from the car, Lynn would scoop a glass of ice and pour the chilled white into the proper wine glass. Then, she would come from around the bar and wait until we rounded the corner to the long hall leading to the lounge area.

"Oh, there's Lynn," Carol would remark with delight, and her steps would always get a little longer and a little faster.

Sometimes, along the way, she would start veering in the direction of the cookie tray, and I would always have to hold her a little tighter.

"After dinner, honey."

Her reply would always come in the form of a furrowed brow. Once we finally reached the lounge area, Lynn would help me get Carol situated on a stool.

"You are too good to me," Carol would say.

"My pleasure, Mrs. Shannon," Lynn invariably replied before giving me a wink. She would pour the wine onto the ice and head around the bar to find something for me. By the time I'd finished the reminiscence, my feet had taken me to 13 Thorn Street. I had walked four miles or so in total, and my body felt good and my heart warm. Though the last couple owners had made some smaller aesthetic changes, the place looked fundamentally the same as it always had. On this quiet morning, I stood in front of our old home remembering Christmases, family gatherings, parties for the football teams, graduation parties, the five of us just sitting in front of the television.

My mind then landed on that birthday night twenty-nine years ago. I saw Carol with her frosted, shoulder-length hair and her stylish fashion. I saw myself with a thick mustache, tight haircut, and a sweater vest. I watched us approach that door with Carol none the wiser. The eruption of joy from our guests, and Carol getting swept into the dining room happened as clearly now as it had back then.

On this chilly morning in the waning days of 2016, instead of taking a right to follow Carol into that large, makeshift dance room full of boozy chatter and laughter, I mentally made a left into our empty living room. I sat down, but not before catching a glimpse of myself. My hair and scruff had gone white, and I'd put on a few pounds since my running days. Like the last fifteen seconds of a song on a record, the sounds of the party faded slowly into silence. I mentally scanned the room and found our old records situated in the wall-sized bookshelf, and the Stobart painting of early Pittsburgh above the fireplace. I spied the couches and chairs, situated in their perfect little spots, and our family pictures scattered around the room. It looked exactly like it did in 1987.

In that silence, I heard something, but it wasn't audible, nor did it come from the constant babble of my mind. It came from within, perhaps even from my soul. It was truth.

I didn't know how to give unconditional love back then.

At the relatively tender age of forty-two, I favored feeding my ambition and having my expectations met, and I hadn't yet attended the retreat at St. Paul's. I was a confident man, to be sure, but I employed a strong will to deny my own imperfections. I spent so many of those years trying to make everything and everyone around me just right. The drive for perfection had created an incredible amount of stress, which often expressed itself in outward agitation. I'd missed the point that nothing was perfect, including me.

Even after St. Paul's, I didn't always embody that enlightenment I'd found, which left me feeling privately ashamed and relying on pride to get me through. Don't get me wrong, during those years between the retreat and the strokes, we celebrated graduations and career successes, enjoyed many anniversaries, and the joys of our life in Hilton Head, but they were also speckled with moments of deep personal guilt. Shame and guilt remind us of our flaws—our lack of perfection. Left untreated, they eat away at one's core. Properly acknowledging and accepting them heals and bolsters the power to love.

All my life, I have been in search of peace. In some ways, I was on the right track in valuing the idea of humility I had discovered in that church library during the retreat. But there's a problem with actively seeking humility: you don't find it; it finds you. It discovered me when I was dealing with a terminal illness and felt ready to give up control of my world, to stop focusing on my own needs and truly focus on Carol's. In so doing, humility freed my soul to accept my life's circumstances as they were, myself for who I was, and Carol for who she was. That was when the joy in my life truly arrived. I wasn't perfect, nor would I ever be. Our life wasn't perfect, but it was wonderful. Perhaps most importantly, I realized that I had a partner in love, a love that had become unconditional.

I could have been a better man back then. I could list the apologies and hugs I wished I had given, but if I was ever going to fully heal, I would need to find a way to forgive myself.

A few days after the seventieth birthday party, Chad paid us a visit. It had gotten to be later in the evening, so I had taken Carol to the master bathroom for her bedtime routine. When it was finished,

I returned to the kitchen to continue talking with my son. We were just discussing the nature of Carol's perseverance when she scooted in from around the corner, standing in her pajamas and holding onto her walker. We kept having our discussion as she approached. Then, when it looked like she was starting to announce something—very much a rarity in those days—we stopped to listen.

"I guess you thought I was going to die or something," she said proudly. "Well, I guess I showed you something. Here I am. Living proof."

She said it better than I ever could. Every time she was knocked down, she got right back up. She'd outlived everyone's expectations, probably even mine. I had begun to wonder if she might even outlive me. She did all this by being the perfect embodiment of the power of perseverance, the inspiration of humility, and the willingness to live each moment as if it was her last. Her strong will to live rekindled a love some forty-plus years beyond its original spark, and she brought her family and a whole community closer.

As Chad and I settled into the brilliance of my wife's words, she proceeded past us and took a seat in her favorite chair in the house. Each time she sat down on her own, she did it the same way. She would get her walker to the side of the chair, shuffle her feet until her body was fully square with the destination, feel for the armrest with her right hand, and then let her backside perform a dramatic freefall into the seat. At impact, her feet would kick up off the ground, and she would ride the momentum to where she could set those little legs on the ottoman in front of her chair. Somehow, she would do all this while simultaneously leaning left to pick up whatever glass happened to be sitting beside the chair. And whether it was water, soda, or wine, she never once spilled a drop.

"Another perfect landing," I said, just like I always did.

"That's all I'm saying," she replied.

The voice of the sea speaks to the soul.
– Kate Chopin

CHAPTER TEN
the mighty fight

February 12, 2017

In that half-second between asleep and awake, I sometimes experienced a moment of prescience. Maybe it came from a life lived in perpetual and generalized worry. On this dark winter morning, it told me I was alone in bed. Startled, I snapped awake and reached for Carol, but came up with a clump of empty sheets.

A loud bang followed.

I flipped the lights on and raced to the bathroom, where I found my wife splayed across the beige tiled floor. Carol had fallen more times than I cared to count, but this instance immediately felt more serious than the rest. I asked her where she felt the pain, and, breathless and wincing, she pointed at her leg and knee.

I ran into the bedroom and called 911. I'd been through this headed-for-the-hospital routine enough to know that they wouldn't let her eat all day just in case they had to do an operation. But since they would have to wean her off the blood thinner for at least a few days, I knew there was zero chance of a surgery happening today anyway. I helped her sit up and went to the kitchen for a bowl of Peanut Butter Puffins, which she dug right into and continued to eat even as the paramedics came through the bathroom door. Soon, we were in the ambulance and off to the hospital. As per usual, I snatched up my brown bag on the way out the door.

By the end of the day, we had another diagnosis to add to Carol's fragile condition: a broken right hip. The news couldn't have been much worse. The way she'd broken the bone, they were going to need to perform an extensive surgery and implant more hardware than she'd ever gotten before. As predicted, they would need a day or so to get her Coumadin pulled back, but they scheduled the surgery for as soon as they could manage.

I spent every minute of the next day with my wife in her hospital room. By nightfall, she couldn't do much more than gaze at the TV

Photo: Carol with son Sean in New York City.

with tired eyes. They had given her some strong pain meds. Just then, I noticed her Valentine's necklace was all bound up, so I pulled the pendant away from the clasp, just like I'd always done.

For the better part of our marriage, as Valentine's Day approached, Carol would ask me how we were going to celebrate the holiday. I would always shrug it off on the basis that it was a made-up holiday. In her usual way, she would accept that answer and say nothing more. Then, on the day of, I would get a little card from her. One year, maybe around 1999, she asked me the same question, and I gave the same response, but I could clearly see that my rejection had hurt her feelings. I thought about it all day, and decided that I'd been harsh about it. If she wanted to have that holiday, why should I get in the way?

We were in Hilton Head, so I went to her favorite shop, a local boutique. The owner of the store didn't wait a second to show me a silver caged heart, which I immediately loved. Apparently, Carol had been eyeing this piece for quite some time. That night, I surprised her with the gift at her favorite restaurant. She beamed all night. Now, with me being among the worst romantics in history, I asked her if she would only wear it on Valentine's Day. In my mind, that would make it extra special. She didn't flinch. Rather, she just nodded in agreement. In retrospect, that was a ridiculous notion. But that's what made Carol so wonderful: my silly rule didn't matter to her. A few years later, I sensed that my request was unreasonable and told her that she could wear it whenever she wanted, which she promptly did. Later still, it turned out that "whenever she wanted" meant "every day."

Now, with another risky surgery looming, I just wanted to see my wife make it through, so she could continue wearing that caged heart whenever she wanted.

When I entered the inpatient surgery waiting room the next morning, I found the massive area packed with patients and their families. On the long wall next to the check-in desk hung four large screens tracking every surgery happening in the hospital. I glanced up at the board. "Carol S," it read. "Pre-op."

I'd been told to expect a three-hour operation, and yet one o'clock came and went, and Carol's status on the board remained "in surgery." Time wore on, and as the crowded room began to thin out, concern settled in. Each hour, the list on the monitors grew smaller, as did the crowd in the waiting room. By 8 P.M., it was just me, an empty board, a quiet room, and my windmill of anxiety. Finally, the call came that they had found a room for Carol on the seventh floor.

To gain access to the wing, I had to press a button and announce my name into the intercom. It felt like an hour before they finally buzzed me in. The moment I burst through her door, Carol looked up at me with those doe eyes of hers.

"What's going on?" she said.

The familiarity of the greeting set me at ease almost immediately. Carol's unabashed casualness always had a way of cutting through my stress. I dragged a reclining chair over to her bed, and for the next couple hours, we held hands and laughed at *Frasier*.

Those past couple days had been full of worry, but as I sat there watching the television, I breathed a gigantic sigh of relief. The first time she'd broken a hip, it took her a solid three months to reach a full recovery. Though I knew it would be a long road to that point again, I could clearly see visions of us heading down the highways and making the most of our seventies. Throughout the evening, I'd thumbed through various websites looking for the right vehicle to make that happen.

We'd done it once before, at the beginning of 2015. A voyage that I often referred to as the best trip of our lives. I'd traded my retirement convertible for an eight-passenger Dodge Ram ProMaster van, which I packed with enough stuff to last us an eternity, including a portable toilet that Carol could use instead of exiting the highway to address her frequent bathroom needs. For an entire month, Carol and I zigzagged through the south visiting friends and family, before ending up in Florida in mid-March to attend an annual symphony fundraiser concert hosted by our dear friends Lori and Juergen.

This particular event happened to fall on the evening before our 46th anniversary, and our last night of that fantastic road trip before heading back to Pittsburgh. After a sunset cocktail hour and a delicious meal, we were treated to the music of some of the world's finest musicians and funniest personalities.

For the last song, the evening's unofficial emcee, violinist Chris Wu, stood and announced to the crowd that in honor of our wedding anniversary, they would play the Irish tune "Danny Boy," a song Juergen knew to be my favorite. I looked over at my wonderful friend, who gestured at me with clasped hands. By the third line, the corners of my eyes were wet with tears. I put my arm around Carol and squeezed her close to me.

I'd probably heard that tune a thousand times in my life. As it draws near the end, both the arrangement and lyrics open up from its restrained and somber reflection on loss to a wide-open expression of love and inner tranquility. For many years, I related more to the melancholy aspect of it, but for a few moments that night, those beautiful notes brought peace to my soul. That wonderful song capped a month-long renewal of our marriage that made us feel more alive and in love than we'd ever been before.

As I sat there in the hospital with Carol, laughing at Niles Crane's antics, I couldn't wait to do it all over again. In the meantime, I vowed to do something special for our anniversary, which was just a month away. It didn't have to be perfect, but I wanted it to be something that reflected Carol's world.

The next morning, I returned to the seventh floor and engaged with the intercom.

"George for Carol Shannon, Room 711."

Silence. In anticipation of being buzzed through, I gave the door a little tug. Still locked.

This can't be good.

My stomach flipped a couple times, and I felt a little dizzy. I hit the intercom button again and announced my presence.

"Mr. Shannon," a man said. "I'll be right out."

An immediate sweat came over me. *No. No. No.*

The overnight nurse came through the door and offered me a seat in the hallway, but I refused. I remember hoping that I was merely in midst of a horrible nightmare. A family brushed past me to enter the wing, reminding me that this was all so real.

"What happened?"

"She needed more and more oxygen through the night," the night nurse reported. "And we gave it to her. But this morning, when I went in to check on her, she was unresponsive."

I must have been in shock, because I didn't say anything. He told me that Carol had been sent down to the medical intensive care unit on the fourth floor. I bolted for the elevator.

"She seemed like such a great woman, sir," he called after me.

Seemed? I thought, noting with dread how he had spoken in the past tense.

On the ride down, I texted Chad. He and Catherine had recently moved back to Pittsburgh, and I knew he could be at the hospital within minutes. The elevator opened to the fourth floor just as I finished the message. I flew for the giant entrance to the unit, its automatic doors swinging open and sparing me the task of having to request permission to enter. I found Carol's name next to the first door on the right. Inside, I encountered more machines than I could count, a sight that sent tense flashbacks to those long days and nights leading up to her heart surgery. The difference was that this unit was the hospital's crisis center. The people they brought here faced death. A commanding young doctor in a white coat proved cool under pressure as she scanned the readings on the machines and issued orders to her incredibly responsive staff. It was immediately clear that the doctor's chief concern was keeping Carol's blood pressure up. In any other situation, I would have cut in to ask the details about what was going on, but from the urgency in everyone's actions, I could sense that this was not the time to intrude. The five minutes it took them to stabilize her might as well have been five years.

The crisis unit's entry doors made a prolonged swooshing sound whenever they swung open, and then rattled to a stop. Every time I heard this sound, I would glance out the door, hoping to see Chad. Eventually the sound heralded his arrival, and soon after came Dr. Ismail. Chad immediately started questioning the doctor who had stabilized my wife, and we learned that no one was quite sure why Carol had become unresponsive. My son set his hand on my shoulder to comfort me, then went into the hall to call his brothers.

"I'm so upset that this happened," Dr. Ismail said as she looked me in the eyes. "Your wife has come through too much to be in this situation. I promise you that I will do everything I can for her. I'll be at her side the whole time."

This remains the most heartfelt and direct thing a doctor has ever said to me. And she kept her word. Dr. Ismail never left Carol's side, and she gave her every chance to live.

Chad returned and informed that Sean would arrive by nightfall, and that Matthew had made a flight reservation for the next morning.

This scenario terrified me well beyond anything she'd gone through; even her heart surgery in 2015 paled in comparison. That time, we'd only been given a sliver of hope for Carol's chances of survival, but even in the bleakest of those hours, I could at least count on that sliver. But now everything felt different. There was an air of finality hanging over the room. It was as if something irrevocable had been set in motion, something that no amount of medical intervention or even the strongest willpower could overcome.

I'd been quite lucky to have spent nearly fifty years with my wife, but I still wasn't ready to see her go, and I worried that she hadn't received all the love she deserved. Sure, I'd poured my love out in the past seven years, but I still had so much to make up for from those times leading up to the strokes. I felt the guilt and shame bubbling to the surface again.

Chad and I sat there all day with our eyes glued to every monitor, looking up only when a doctor or nurse arrived to check on Carol's vitals. Had it really been less than twelve hours since my wife and I had been laughing at some predictable mess that Niles Crane had gotten himself into? At some point, she seemed like she was starting to respond to our voices, but she didn't open her eyes or speak. The good news was that she'd remained stable the rest of the day. By the time Sean arrived that night, she had been sound asleep for several hours, so we all went home to get some rest.

The next morning, we arrived to a pleasant surprise. Carol was awake, though groggy, and clearly trying to speak with us. It was tough to understand most of what she said, but there was one thing she made clear: she didn't want the ventilator. The number of F-bombs she dropped while tugging on her tubes made it impossible to mistake her meaning. I understand why. That thing plunging down her throat looked painful. I couldn't imagine having to live with something like that. As much as she hated that machine, we weren't yet sure if she would survive without it.

The familiar swoosh and rattle of the door announced Dr. Ismail's entry into the ICU. She arrived with her standard confidence and upbeat tone, but it didn't last long. Carol's blood pressure took another nosedive. Dr. Ismail didn't hesitate to take charge of the situation. She directed nurses, specialists, and other physicians until the intensivist could arrive from working on another patient in critical condition. Moments after the latter doctor arrived, Carol's blood pressure fell through the floor. She had suffered a full-fledged cardiac event. They called for the crash cart and pushed us from the room.

I objected, wanting to be next to that bed so I could beg my wife not to leave. A few minutes later, Dr. Ismail rushed out. They'd saved Carol but needed urgent approval to place a heart pump. Without it, she would pass away. The procedure itself could cause a whole host of complications. The decision seemed obvious. Live to fight another day. Chad and Sean agreed.

I paced and paced for the next sixty minutes. A dozen eternities later, when the surgeon came through those doors and flashed a smile, I let go the longest sigh of relief I'd ever breathed. I hadn't lost my Carol.

The hospital would be moving her to the Cardiac Intensive Care Unit, or CCU, on the eleventh floor. The staff warned that she would likely be staying there for a long stretch. The preceding day and a half had been a whirlwind, and while the inevitability of death hadn't disappeared, at least it had receded.

The heart pump granted Carol's body a chance to heal, and the medical staff an extension of time to figure things out. "So, I guess Carol decided to throw us another curveball today," Dr. Ismail said with a chuckle.

The curveballs would continue. My wife, bedridden and snaked with more wires than a server room, was doing her best Sandy Koufax impression, just one nasty breaking ball after another.

Most likely because of the trauma of the previous day, the circulation in Carol's left leg suddenly stopped, causing it to blow up like a balloon. The situation became emergent even before we had a chance to settle in and think about it. The next thing I knew, a team of doctors from the vascular surgery department was handing me an onslaught of papers highlighting the benefits of surgery (staying alive), and mundanely rushing through the downside (the possible loss of a leg and the risks of amputation surgery).

I couldn't count the number of times a similar scenario had played out during my wife's care, but no matter how often I'd faced these situations, it always seemed strange that I would need to read a comprehensive legal document and provide a signature while under such incredible duress. Every time, I disregarded the rehearsed words delivered by the doctor or resident and signed my name as quickly as I could. If whatever they wanted to do was going to give Carol a chance, then they could count me on board every time.

Soon after, the doctors were making several deep incisions into Carol's leg, acting quickly to get her veins in working order. In this way, the medical team managed to foul off that first breaking ball.

For the rest of that first week, things seemed headed in the right direction. They'd identified Carol's mitral valve as the likely culprit in causing all the heart problems. Apparently, whenever that valve starts leaking, it can cause all sorts of problems. The initial plan was to see if the picture would improve with time and medicine, and for a few days, it seemed to work. But then came the next big step. Carol would need to wean off the ventilator. Much to everyone's surprise, she met this challenge just a couple days later.

When the nursing staff brought us back in to see her, we swarmed around her bed, all of us eager to hear how she felt.

"Having that tube out's got to feel good, huh?" Matthew said.

"Get me out of here," Carol said.

Totally understandable proposition, I thought.

"How you feeling, Mama?" Sean said.

We all knew the answer.

"I'm fine," she said.

When I leaned in to give her a kiss, she looked up at me intently.

"Can I go now?"

"They still need to do a little more work," I said.

She snarled playfully as she turned her attention to Chad. "He's just mad because I have a boyfriend."

None of us had any idea who the mysterious interloper could be, but we all had a good laugh.

"I'm serious."

I told her she could have whatever she wanted, which seemed to calm her down. Before we left that night, I kissed her three times on the forehead and told her that the triple kiss would be how she would know it was me. She shot me a fatigued but genuine smile, and gave me a couple long bats of her lashes—a quick flirt, if I wasn't mistaken. I can't properly express how great it was to have her back. I even let visions of us taking on the open roads flash back into my mind. She'd beaten the odds on everything else; why not this one, too?

Less than twenty-four hours later, Carol delivered her next curveball. The staff discovered that she wasn't getting enough oxygen, so the hospitalist was forced to put her back on the ventilator.

The medical team was puzzled as they called for the X-ray machine. A deep respiratory infection delivered the nastiest curveball yet by filling Carol's lungs with fluid. A particularly insidious complication was that the best chance of improving an infection was to get up and move around—the one thing my wife wasn't anywhere near equipped to do.

With exercise impossible, and with the pills failing to improve Carol's condition, we now found ourselves considering riskier alternatives. Everyone seemed to agree that open heart surgery was completely out of the question, as it would be too much for an already overtaxed body. The last, best hope involved reaching the damaged mitral valve with the use of a catheter guided through her femoral artery. But she would need to get much better before anyone would even consider the measure. So now we had been backed into a wait-and-see approach.

Over the next couple weeks, Carol would send a steady stream of tough pitches at the medical staff, and they would battle her right back to keep the at-bat alive. Just as her infection started to look better, her diabetes roared out of control, hampering her kidneys. Her blood pressure came down, but her body retained fluids. Lasix drained the fluids, but then her blood pressure crept below the low end of normal. No matter what the medical staff did, Carol never seemed to come out ahead.

After three weeks, Carol's doctors started to worry that the ventilator would have to remain in permanently. Although Carol had demonstrated a few moments of mental coherence over the past couple weeks, her speech was becoming rarer and less rational. In her confusion, she would pull at her many lines and tubes. Eventually they outfitted her with wrist restraints. The infection had improved modestly, but it lingered like an unwanted guest. To make matters worse, her unstable blood pressure hung over her like a ticking clock.

Before I knew it, we had rolled into March. Our wedding anniversary was less than two weeks away. By this point, that glimmer of hope I'd experienced after her heart-pump procedure had begun to flicker as if burning out. The thought of road trips landed in the category of wild-eyed dreams. I would have done anything for her to beat this breathing machine situation, to get her feeling half-normal and on to rehab so she could regain some strength. If we could just get her home, I would rearrange everything in our lives to make the best of it—for however long that might be.

Almost every discipline in the Cardiovascular Institute of Allegheny General Hospital had consulted on my wife's case. We must have had a dozen conversations at the foot of her bed or just outside her door. The choice eventually came down to either letting the matter continue in this way, which would mean that she would likely never come off the ventilator and would be permanently bedridden, or we could take the chance for a better quality of life by trying to solve the valve issue. Though her health wasn't ideal, the doctors believed that she was at least stable enough to give her a fighting chance to survive an interventional procedure.

As her healthcare power of attorney, the final decision fell to me.

The only sound as I looked down at her was the steady beat of the ventilator. I'd been married to Carol for nearly fifty years, so I knew that she would want to live, but at the same time, I tried to imagine her riding out her final years in a hospital bed set up in our bedroom. Would she be happy?

Never, I thought.

She hated the walker with a passion, and the wheelchair even more so. Suddenly it seemed so clear. She would want to get back on her feet, or not at all.

On March 5th, I made the decision to move ahead. All we needed was a one good day of stability before the doctors could clear her for the procedure. Remarkably, despite the wide array of potential problems, March 7th went off stunningly well.

Late into the evening, the boys and I took turns at the head of the bed, stroking Carol's hair and whispering our own personal brands of encouragement. Dr. Ismail came into the room and explained the plan for the next day. As always, she finished by checking with Carol. My wife looked at me, and I nodded. Ever the one to go my way, Carol responded to the doctor in kind. After Dr. Ismail cleared out, I asked the boys for a few minutes alone with their mother.

All the delicate talk of death and last-ditch efforts instilled such incredible fear in me. Though the medical facts had been piling up, I remained steadfast against the possibility that she might not survive. At this point, I wanted just one more day at home, to set up her breakfast and pills one last time. I would bargain anything to load her back into the car for a final swing through the doctors' appointments, her comedy routine at rehab, and the largest fucking box of popcorn in the movie theater; one more chance for me to fall asleep watching TV and have her wake me up by asking if I was awake.

When my sons and I got home that night, I somehow managed to fall asleep. According to those big red numbers on the ceiling, it was 1:07 A.M. when my phone rang. I let out a yell as I snapped awake. The number on my phone I recognized immediately as a call from the hospital. There was nothing I could imagine wanting to do less than pick up that line.

An oddly excited man who identified himself as the night doctor told me that Carol had pulled out her ventilator tube. While I'm still not sure to this day whether I felt more dread than confusion over that statement, his next announcement mystified me to the core. She was breathing perfectly fine on her own. No tube. No machine. Nothing.

I sat on the edge of my bed for a long while, trying to wrap my head around what I'd just learned. My first reaction after hanging up was to tell Chad that we needed to go to the hospital because this doctor must have had his facts wrong. Plus, I'd forgotten to ask how she'd done it. We had been told for weeks that Carol couldn't survive without oxygen assistance. We had seen her backslide into respiratory distress at least once on lower levels of support. It just didn't add up, and I wanted answers.

By the next morning, the whole medical staff was abuzz about Carol's feat. Halfway into cleaning up my wife's bedclothes, the night nurse had been pulled from the room on an emergency. Less than three minutes later, all the bells and whistles had sounded from Carol's room. When a group of nurses arrived to address the chaos, Carol had the ventilator mask in her hand, her wrist restraints perfectly strapped.

Then, like the critical scene in a detective picture, all the requisite evidence flashed before my eyes. Fact one: Carol had been stretching her left arm every which way for the past several days, and only now did I realize that she'd been testing the limits of her restraints. Fact two: Carol waited until the perfect moment, when her pillows weren't propping her up and nobody had eyes on her. Fact three: The moment she was alone, Carol had laid herself prone and shimmied down the bed to the point where her hand could reach the tube plunging down her throat.

I have two views on this event, and they aren't mutually exclusive. I'll call the first one the Sinatra Theory. Every doctor on that unit had stood within earshot of Carol as they explained her ongoing medical saga. The ventilator had further hampered an already quiet person, but her mind and hearing had remained needle-sharp. So, just two days prior, when we were all in the hallway putting this risky proposition on the table, Carol decided that she was going to flip that table, with all its delicate medical ideas, right upside down. She'd had enough sutures, procedures, tubes, and machines for a lifetime. If taking away the artificial oxygen supply would end it, then so be it. And just like one of her favorite Sinatra songs, she was going to do it her way.

The second theory, a much more difficult one to verify, operates more like a supplement to the first. It goes like this: Carol and I had built up some goodwill with God, given Carol's lifetime of kindness, our frequent trips to church, and my consistent post-communion discussions from the kneeler. Even to this day, I wonder whether somewhere in her struggle to get hold of the ventilator, Carol was assisted by God. She'd made peace with her Creator and got a little help in fulfilling her desire to remove that cumbersome thing. I can't quote more than a line or two of scripture, have always kept my religion private, and don't know whether I'm going to heaven or hell, but that event made me see faith in a whole new way.

Either way, Carol's great escape was an extraordinary thing. When I was finally able to visit with her, she would only give that feeble little shoulder shrug when I questioned her on what she was thinking. Then it hit me like the proverbial ton of bricks. Carol had effectively delivered her signature move, the left-arm shoulder shrug punctuated by an upturned palm—a blend of "it is what it is" and "you left me no choice."

The longer I sat there, the less I tried to understand her actions, and the more I let myself be amazed by them. Then, in that cleaned slate of my mind, I remembered a self-selected nugget of wisdom etched into my book of quotes:

"The more we feel our lives count for something, the less we fear death."

With her late-night hospital bed acrobatics, Carol had announced that she was ready to let the cards fall where they may. But she had also helped me. She'd let me know that my work was done—that it was okay to let go.

The desire to have one last day with her at home largely came from the deepest part of my heart. I didn't want to lose my soulmate. Some small part of it also came from my lifelong struggle to want things to work out in a perfect little way, to get her home for just one more perfect day. I wanted her to live forever, so I could keep showing her how much I loved her, but she showed me that her life had been full, and that it counted for something. The fear of her death wasn't hers, but mine. If she was willing to let life play out, I needed to be just as willing.

Time is but the stream I go a-fishing in. I drink at it;
but while I drink I see the sandy bottom
and detect how shallow it is.
Its thin current slides away, but eternity remains

– Henry David Thoreau
Walden

CHAPTER ELEVEN
on her own two feet

March 14, 2017

Even though I'd spent almost every waking moment at the hospital, every time I walked into Carol's room, I had to pinch myself. Without the ventilator for almost a week, she was headed to the step-down unit, the next and final step before being discharged. She'd done so well that Sean and Matthew had returned to their regular lives in New York and Montana. When she saw me enter, she offered a little wave and tilted her head in a signal that she wanted a kiss on the cheek. I strolled over and gave it gladly.

Even though it was a day early, I couldn't wait any longer. I pulled the chair next to her bed to tell her about her anniversary gift. But before I could say anything, a doctor I hadn't seen before slipped into the room to announce the next curveball.

"Excuse me, sir," the young man said. "I think one of your wife's teeth has fallen into her lung."

I regarded the doctor a little cross-eyed and went to Carol, who'd already opened her mouth to let me inspect. Dread washed over me as I bent down and examined her teeth like a dentist. I'd been so ready to see my wife take the next step toward getting home, and I knew how desperate she'd become to leave, so a setback on something so unexpected would have been devastating. Just as I was set to quit looking, I noticed a gap, and asked Carol to open wider.

"Well I'll be damned," I said. "There's one missing."

Carol would need to head down to the imaging lab to verify the doctor's theory. I agreed to the procedure, and off they went with my wife. I would have to wait to share her gift with her.

Not too long after Carol's strokes, a nonprofit group in Sewickley announced plans to build a little two-screen movie theater in town. My wife was beside herself at this news, and she urged me to get involved with the project. Life had gotten too busy for me to follow up on it. Around the time we moved from the hills back to the village,

---

Photo: Carol with George and son Matthew at wedding in Pittsburgh.

they'd started excavating the grounds. It was official—our new home would be located less than a hundred yards from an endless supply of popcorn, Diet Coke, and movies.

Finally, eighteen months after breaking ground, the Tull Family Theater (named so after a very generous donation) was set to open in mid-January 2017. Carol counted down the days until the opening, and I couldn't wait to walk her through those doors for the first time. A few small hiccups later, and the opening had been postponed until February 17, 2017, right as Carol had begun her long hospitalization.

I'd felt so bad that she couldn't make the premiere. On the way to the hospital one morning, I swung by the theater with a question for the front office and got just the answer I wanted. My special gift for Carol was in the bag. As I made my way out of the building, a wall full of plaques caught my eye. Those who had contributed money to the project had their names inscribed on these beautiful silver-gray tablets. I turned around, explained the situation to the staff in the office, and one check later, the number of anniversary gifts had doubled.

When they wheeled her into the room after her X-ray session, the doctor confirmed that her tooth was indeed in her lung, and that the bronchoscope would be necessary since that tooth could turn into something of an infection magnet. More risks explained, more papers signed, and we were scheduled for an anniversary day procedure. Compared to many of the twists and turns over the past month, this bend didn't raise too much concern. But considering Carol's fragile condition, I realized that it could be a stumbling block.

Not wanting to wait a second longer, I went back to the bedside. "The new movie theater opened."

"Oh, did it really?" she exclaimed. The little spark I'd seen in her eye returned, the same one I'd seen on the day the theater was first announced.

"They're hiring for certain jobs," I told her. "And the one they need most is ticket-takers. Any interest?"

Carol blinked at me and confirmed her interest. "I'd like that a lot." She gazed into my eyes in a way I hadn't seen in what felt like years.

"Well," I said, laying it on thick, "I can't make any guarantees, but I'm in good with the management there."

She squeezed my hand tight and leveled me with an intense stare. "I want the fucking job."

I laughed, but not entirely because of the profanity. What a relief to hear her string together a coherent five-word sentence. It had been a long time. "I also finally donated to the theater," I said. "Just like you always wanted me to."

I'd stopped by the theater that morning to get a cell phone snapshot of the freshest names on the wall of plaques: Carol and George Shannon. I handed her the phone and helped her hold it up.

"Happy Anniversary."

She took a long look, and with her eyes watering, said, "You're too good to me."

Impossible, I thought.

The next morning, they performed the bronchoscope and removed the tooth without a hitch. The doctor who performed the procedure told me that it was the fastest one he'd ever done, and that it might have beaten the hospital record. She'd thrown her last curveball.

Ten days later, we would be packing up Carol's things and heading for Villa St. Joseph ("The Villa"), a skilled nursing facility not too far down the Ohio River from where we lived. Over that week and a half, the doctors did they best they could, but some lingering issues remained, like the slowly healing incisions and the quarrelsome respiratory infection. At the time we left the hospital, our biggest hurdle to getting Carol home was the rehabilitation of her significantly weakened body. I'd come to grips with the prospect that if Carol got home, her return would probably be brief, but I hung onto that hope as I followed that ambulance down the highway to the rehab facility.

The Villa resides on the grounds of a convent called the Sisters of St. Joseph motherhouse, an institution in Baden and the rest of Western Pennsylvania for over a hundred years. Within minutes after entering through the front door, I felt an overwhelming sense of warmth and knew that my wife was in the right place.

As they got Carol situated, I wandered the facilities. They were modest, but full of kind and attentive staff members. More than that, I felt a keen sense of peace being in a place full of so many people devoted to their faith. When it came time for me to see my wife, they escorted me into her new room. It was a small and private space that immediately took me right to the spring of 1969, when Carol and I rented our first apartment together.

At the time, Carol was a booking agent with TWA, and we were looking for a place to live as we prepared for our upcoming wedding. We couldn't afford much, and finding inexpensive housing in Pittsburgh was a tough task. We'd looked everywhere from East Liberty to Bethel Park, a large swath of real estate twenty or so miles long. Four months into our search, we caught wind of a one-bedroom for ninety bucks a month in a little town called Pleasant Hills.

On the day of the showing, I arrived first, and the agent and I had to wait on Carol. She would wear these little stub-heels for work, and they made a clicking sound on the floor loud enough for us to hear from down the hall. She strolled in, cig in hand, with a fresh haircut and a new cashmere coat. The agent showed us around the little one-bedroom, which didn't take long, since, apart from the bedroom, there was only a small bathroom off the dining/kitchen/living room combo. The place was maybe a total of eight hundred square feet.

"Well?" the agent said. "What do you think?"

Carol's heels clicked a small circle around the main room as she nodded in approval. Then, she took a long drag from her cigarette and spun a perfect pirouette to face us. "Let's talk turkey," she said, the smoke trailing from her lips.

More than ever before, I knew in that moment that I loved her. That moment was a bottle of the essence of my wife, a bottle from which I still drink every now and then.

We ended up taking the place for the listed price.

I sat next to my wife and stroked her hand while we waited for the care team to explain the plan. In the quietness of those few minutes, I felt deeply comforted by the crucifix I spotted above the door. In our master bedroom, no matter where Carol and I lived, we always hoisted a cross—one that I'd gotten from the church way back when I had rheumatic fever.

The projected course of rehabilitation was that it would last at least a month, and that was just to get her back to the point where she could do the very basic things like sitting up in bed, standing up from a seated position, and walking short distances. They took it very easy for the first couple days, and would end the session after they'd gotten her to sit up on the edge of the bed for a minute. Six weeks in the prone position had caused her body to deteriorate to the point where even her sitting muscles were like gel.

Even the most minimal amount of exertion wore Carol out, which was to be expected considering what she'd gone through. It seemed that all she really wanted to do was sleep. A couple days after her admission to the nursing facility, Chad and Catherine paid her a visit. Even though they'd arrived just after dinnertime, Carol had already zonked out. They taped a small Pittsburgh Penguins flag under her crucifix before they left. The Stanley Cup playoffs were a couple weeks away, and they figured she'd bring the team luck. One week into Carol's stay, on the last day of March, the physical therapy staff started using a machine to help her stand from the edge of the bed. This gadget had a handlebar to grab while she pulled herself up, along with the guiding help of the therapist's hands. Though I hoped for success, I had my doubts, as I'd seen Carol struggle to stand for months, even before her long hospital stay. With the nursing staff firmly supporting her backside, Carol nailed it on her first try. Her tenacity filled me with pride and admiration. Time and again, she'd proved to us that her will had the tensile strength of steel. For the next three days, she made more and more progress, standing for just a few seconds longer. Though she'd never utter a gripe, I could tell it hurt like hell.

On April 4th, she had her biggest day yet. For starters, we were able to get her dressed for the first time since this whole ordeal had begun. Since she had these bright yellow, slip-resistant socks on, I brought in a matching Penguins shirt from the previous year's Stanley Cup Championship. Sean had become such a huge fan over the years, and Carol had gotten caught up in his excitement and had become a fan too. With her standard black athletic pants, she was ready for the first playoff series of 2017, now just about a week away.

As a bonus, Chad had driven out from Pittsburgh to see her before he left for a trip with his father-in-law.

After lunch, the therapy team came into Carol's room with their machine. By this point in the day, she'd been taken out of bed and placed in a bedside chair. When they brought the machine over, she pushed herself to the edge of the chair. Clearly, she wanted this exercise over with as quickly as possible. Device in place, she put her hands around the little bar and pulled herself up about halfway before she stopped cold. We joined the two therapists in their words of encouragement. Her legs shook, and it appeared that she might sit down, but eventually, with a cross face and all her effort, she pulled herself up on her own. For a few wonderful seconds, and for the first time in nearly two months, Carol had gotten back on her own two feet.

Chad and I popped out of our chairs in excitement, practically high-fiving each other. I wanted to hug my wife, but the therapists were in the process of sitting her back down. She vehemently rejected doing another round, and they didn't push the matter. We tried to take her into the television room, but a few minutes later, she asked to be put back to bed.

After they turned out the lights, my son went to kiss his mother on the forehead and told her, "I love you, and don't you ever forget it." The next morning, I met with one of the house doctors to get an update. Just before we went into Carol's room, I told her about how much my wife loved the movies and about the anniversary gifts I'd given her. After her examination, the doctor leaned against the bed and grabbed Carol's hand.

"We're going to get you home," she said. "And you're going to go to that movie theater, get a box of popcorn and a big Diet Coke, and watch as many movies as you want."

To that wonderful personal touch, she added the warmest smile I'd ever seen from a doctor. It was infectious, but Carol's expression remained as steely as her will.

"And I want that fucking job," she blasted as she pointed her finger at me.

My wife and I spent the day together. Night soon fell, and Carol followed suit with her quick trip into sleep. Before I left, I gave her my customary three kisses like I had done every night since I'd almost lost her in the hospital.

I'd come back from the Villa and was having a glass of wine when I received a text from Matthew saying, "Hi, Mom." Along with the text, he'd attached a photo of himself sitting on his boat, which he'd pulled onto the edge of a beautiful river in Montana, snow-capped mountains in the background. Carol loved nothing more than she loved her children. It would be the first thing I would show her in the morning when I returned.

The phone rang and buzzed, and the reliable red numbers on my ceiling informed that it was 4:15 A.M. Even though Carol had only been a resident for ten days, I already recognized the Villa's number. I knew that I should let that call go to voicemail, and wanted to throw that phone into the trash, because I knew that the news couldn't be anything but terrible.

I will never forget the words of that conversation, but they are too painful to share. The essence was that Carol had been found unresponsive again, and that there was no time to send her all the way down to AGH, so they had to send her to our local hospital in Sewickley, which was about four blocks from our home. I fumbled through getting dressed, but I eventually made it out the door.

For reasons still unknown, I left my car behind in favor of taking the route on foot. I also left my trusty brown bag I'd taken with me on every emergency. At 4:30 A.M., not a single store had opened, and I'd beaten everyone to the sidewalks. Just me and the streets of Sewickley. The only stoplight in town sits at the corner of Beaver and Broad Streets. From that corner, no matter which direction you look, you can see so much of my last thirty-seven years with Carol.

To reach the hospital from where I live, you make a left up the hill at Broad Street until you reach the end of it, which is where the Emergency Room is located. As I hoofed along Beaver and neared the left turn, I heard a vehicle coming up Broad, which connects with the highway that takes you to the Villa. When I turned my head right, I saw an ambulance rolling up the road at a casual rate of speed, with no lights and no signs of urgency. I came to a stop under the traffic light, turned my gaze left, and watched the tail lights of the big white truck until it turned toward the ER.

If I made a right at the light and ran as hard as I could for the next quarter mile, I would come upon St. James Church, where I'd spent many Saturday nights at the pew of negotiations. Maybe the doors would be open, and before the paramedics brought her into the hospital, I could get back down on my knees and make a last-minute deal. There was nothing I wouldn't offer. Instead, I closed my eyes and honed in on the panic that had gripped my heart so tightly. There was nothing I could do to change the outcome.

In that kind of quiet, you can hear the click of the stoplight as it changes. I don't know how many rotations I let pass by before I exhaled the sour fear from my body and took my first steps toward the hospital. The distance from that corner to the sliding emergency doors can't be any more than two hundred yards, but it felt like the longest climb I've ever endured. And it wasn't because of the looming sadness—that would come later. When your brain processes the implications of loss, it sends a flood of memories, perhaps to ease the pain. In the span of two and a half blocks, it's like you've lived forty-seven-some-odd years all over again.

CHAPTER TWELVE
for the rest of my years

For you will bend and tell me that you love me, and
I shall sleep in peace until you come to me!
– Frederic Weatherly
lyrics from "Danny Boy"

June 12, 2017

We laid Carol to rest two months ago. Almost every day since then, I've gotten up first thing in the morning to walk the streets of Sewickley. I make that same left at the corner of Beaver and Broad, but now I go past the hospital on my way to the only land beyond it: the Sewickley Cemetery, a beautiful patch of rolling hills with a view of the Ohio River. Though I don't want to think about it, each time I pass the Emergency Room, my mind takes me right back to that terrible April morning.

In the last seven years, I'd been to the ER a dozen times, but that morning in April was the first occasion on which they took me back as soon as I arrived. For a split second, I'd held out hope that Carol hadn't been the one riding in that unhurried ambulance. But I knew the truth of it almost immediately, because they escorted me to a private sitting room with a couch and a dimly lit lamp—a place that looked like the lounge in a funeral parlor. A minute or so later, the gentlest of doctors broke the news to me. My Carol was gone.

I wish I could say that when I entered the room to say my final goodbye, I was comforted by the peace on her face, a sight I hadn't seen in months. But the truth is that I had to fight back the impulse to ask the medical staff to try at least once more to revive her, to let me hear one last one-liner, see one more shoulder shrug, or have one more chance to tell her how much I loved her. Through my tears, I apologized to her for not showing her more love like I should have, and I waited in vain for the answer to my repeated question of how I could live without her. I stayed with Carol for another two hours,

---

Photo: Carol hugging George.

137

holding her hand as tightly as I could. Before I left, I removed her caged-heart necklace. I have worn it every moment since.

On this morning, I awoke only slightly less than crippled by the heavy sadness I'd been feeling since the day Carol died. For weeks beyond her death, I found myself still gripped with the question of whether I'd done enough for her, and whether I'd made her feel the love to the best of my power. Lately, I'd been able to quell those thoughts with the remembrance of so many moments we'd shared during the rejuvenation of our marriage, or when the doubts lingered, by conjuring up the memory of her voice telling me that she loved her Pogey. This day, the trip up the winding road that connects the edge of the village to the main part of the cemetery felt a little easier.

I enjoyed the shady stroll among the bantering birds, and was calmed by the prospect that in a few short minutes, I would be having my morning conversation with my wife. I couldn't wait to tell her that the Penguins had won the Stanley Cup the previous night, something she rooted for but really wouldn't have cared about at all. Rather, she would have adored the fact that the boys and I kept her spirit alive and fed off an unspoken connection to her during the two months of the playoff run. She would be proud and delighted to know that, even in her passing, she had managed to bring the family closer.

Located in the middle of the cemetery, the stone and glass mausoleum where Carol now resides contains a forty-seat chapel and two walls for entombment. I arrived to find it empty, and entered the still room. As always, I took the chair closest to my wife. I'd chosen an interior tomb because I didn't want her to be cold or get wet, or otherwise be exposed to earth. I wanted her to stay warm and comfortable until I met her in there one day. As I gazed into the clean, white slab where her name had been inscribed, I told myself that she would have liked my choice—but then again, she would've agreed with me no matter what.

My name had also been inscribed on that plaque, just beneath hers, and there was no place that I desired to be more than in my own silver urn touching her matching urn. I knew that if that were the case, then I would get to see her bright smile again, hold that little hand once more, and buy her more boxes of popcorn. Instead, we continued to be separated by a cosmic gap that, since her death, had been filled most often with a sadness proportionate to the profound love that had grown between us over the past seven years.

On each wall of the mausoleum there are forty or so vaults, each with a marble footer separating the tombs from the floor. Under my wife's resting place, I had placed an orchid. Though she loved many different flowers, the orchid was always Carol's favorite. For as long as I could remember, she'd brought that notoriously fussy floral wonder into our home and kept it alive with tender attention and care. Even up to the week before she'd taken her final fall, Carol insisted on being helped around the condo to tend to her orchids. She'd shed them of their dried leaves to keep them thriving, and she always knew when to feed them just the right amount of water.

After I updated her about how she'd kept her grieving family close for the past couple months, I fetched some water for her orchid. Then, like every other time I'd come up to visit her, I sat with my thoughts and memories. I'd traded my place of daily reflection from the edge of the bed in my condo for a seat next to where Carol had been enshrined.

I drifted into this session of deliberation by thinking of Carol's quippish personality. I had often wondered whether her provocative ways were a result of the strokes—that somehow the filter in Carol's mind had been stripped away by the brain injury, which left us with a new Carol. But as the years passed, and as I lightened up, I understood it in an entirely different light. The woman with whom I'd spent these past several years was the true Carol. She had just come into her own. The later-in-life wife of mine spoke her piece, got angry with me, disagreed with me, and even teased me. All the while, this once-unassuming woman who would've rather drowned than speak publicly had developed a keen sense of comedic timing, sharpened her wit, and ultimately captured every room.

Even deeper than what made her so entertaining was that she had become clear in what she wanted. That had manifested itself when she pulled at her first tube in the hospital and had carried through until she yanked out her ventilator weeks before her death. In between, she'd offered sharp opinions about the things important to her, from the size of the box of popcorn to her utter distaste for physical therapy.

Through it all, she'd let her inner self shine, particularly the two qualities that had always defined her: selflessness and tenacity. Though she'd defined boundaries like she never had before, she still deferred to others in matters that weren't important to her, and she never lost sight of the sacrifices that many had made on her behalf. She always acknowledged those sacrifices with a "You're too good to me," or a

"Thank you for all you do." With a disability to lean on, it would have been so easy for her to have made her remaining days all about herself, or to wallow in self-pity. Not Carol. She'd gone the opposite way, taking great pains to avoid talking about her condition, and even asking me from time to time whether she'd become a burden. More than anything, she just wanted to live life as she always had.

Our decision to remain undeterred in our daily routine had made our new existence quite public. The slow and steady entrances we'd made wherever we went drew attention from people we knew, and from people we didn't know. I often found myself presented with an honest inquiry or compassionate sentiment about how hard taking care of Carol must have been. These questions and comments had always caught me off guard. From day one, I'd seen my efforts as the critical marriage vow, in sickness and in health, as something honorable, and as something I wanted to do even when it became stressful at times. After years of reflection, it all makes sense to me now. Though I didn't know it back when people would say these otherwise well-intended things to me, this had been my evolution into unconditional love.

Though they could've never known the necessary personal journey to a renewed humility I'd taken to get there, they were simply observing the love between us. By giving my life over to my wife's, I'd knocked out my lifelong defenses and opened myself up to the possibility of unconditional love. Each day I worked to make her happy and get the most out of her life, the more fulfilled my own life became. The better I felt about life, the more I wanted to do for Carol, and the deeper into love I fell.

I'll freely admit that at first it felt like I'd been left in a forest with no map. A lifetime of plans, dreams, and visions of retirement vanished in a single month. My kids and most of my extended family had all moved away, and I lived in a disabled-unfriendly home with no idea about how to be a caregiver. As I stood in that dense forest, I had two choices: sit down and wait for help, or choose one of the many paths and follow it to its conclusion. I decided that my path would be to find the good. When I took my first steps, I had no idea that my trail would lead me to a panoramic view of life itself, with the peaks of unconditional love and valleys of humility. But that ends up being the point, after all. I'd discovered the chance to shower my wife with love, to challenge myself at an older age, and to enjoy many more hearty laughs than I'd ever thought possible.

Of course there is also the community of support that one can have in these situations. Words of encouragement from friends, family, and even total strangers served as critical fuel for my self-esteem as a caregiver. The smiles we received in church after communion, the little affirmative nods in the restaurants we frequented, or the slaps on the back from my closest buddies kept the motors running. In those darker moments, when the flames of fatigue and worry threatened to knock me down, it was the generous compliments that helped me through.

Perhaps the biggest moment of encouragement came from one of the most unexpected places. One day, not long before Carol passed, I ran into Sister Mary Eileen, the former principal of the parochial school my kids had attended, and invited her up to dinner.

During dinner, my feelings of disconnection from the church and guilt over my lack of service grew worse in the presence of this dedicated religious woman. As we moved onto coffee, someone took Carol to the bathroom, and I leaned in to my company to share a thought that had been plaguing me for some time. I was nervous, as the good nun still carried an air of authority, even decades after she'd retired.

"I don't feel as though I'm being a very good Catholic."

Now, all my life, I believed that appropriate worship of a higher being required that I attend church, follow its rules, and give financial help when I could. I lived most of my life that way. But I couldn't count how many Sunday Masses Carol and I had missed after she got sick. And even though we'd make it back, there was nothing routine about our attendance.

The tough but big-hearted nun set her eyes on mine. "What's eating at you, dear?"

"You know," I said, "it really bothers me that I haven't been to church much over these past few years."

Her gaze grew stern. I imagined how her students must have responded to this, because she certainly captured my attention. Her spine went rigid, and with one sturdy finger, she tapped the table and let me have it.

"You don't worry about that!" She searched my eyes for any confusion about her instruction. "You're doing God's work right here." Her expression warmed as she waited until my gaze met hers.

Just like that, she'd lifted a heavy and self-inflicted burden from

141

my mind. At first, I also felt quite honored that this esteemed woman of the cloth would consider me as having done God's work. Up to that point, I hadn't considered taking care of my wife as something entirely Christian by nature, but it did make sense that I'd have been more effective with the message by helping my wife than I'd have been sitting in a pew once a week for fifty minutes or so.

Sister Mary Eileen's kind words made me feel as though I was making a difference in my wife's life. And it's true, no matter what I've done, I've always pursued meaning. I suspect that if I'd gutted out my first job as a teacher, I'd have found that job to be extremely rewarding. When, as a young man, I finally landed with the right sales job, I loved that territory because it had basically zero sales. I got to make the region grow for twenty-two years before moving on to another challenge.

While Carol's new situation was unfolding, I wanted to make a difference in her life in some way. And as the dust settled, it became clear that the number one thing I could do would be to try to maintain her quality of life. With a purpose in mind, I used that goal as a guiding force in almost every decision, from where we lived, to how we ate, to how we traveled, to what we did for entertainment. Undoubtedly, that's how I'd gotten my start, but that's not how we finished.

Like most other lessons I've learned in life, the real import of the message that night took a long time to settle in. All along, there was something bigger at work, something I didn't recognize until after Carol was gone. Sure, I'd started out trying to make a difference in her life, and I'm not too humble to agree that, all-in-all, I'd made it an enjoyable ride for those final years. But in her quiet and inconspicuous way, Carol had been the one to take me on the journey, and to transform me into a better man in the process. I'd gone far afield from the enlightened young man ready to take on the world and seek true humility following the St. Paul's retreat. In pouring my entire focus onto Carol, I'd found my way back and discovered an internal peace through living the life of a humble man. In the end, we'd taken care of each other, and in the process, our marriage had reached a serenity we'd never imagined.

The orchid sitting below Carol's crypt had come from one of the many that had been delivered to the funeral home after her passing. On the day of her committal service, I'd brought up a beautiful white one with a faint purple pattern and put it in the same place where it sits today. Nearly every day, I've come up to talk to her and take care of her flower. Though I've tried my best, my thumb isn't nearly as green as my wife's. In the two months since Carol's passing, all but one petal has fallen to the floor. Though that last one's still hanging on, it is dried and curled. Time will soon consume the last moments of the flower's life, and this lingering vestige of my connection to my wife will then be gone. I've wanted nothing more than to see that plant survive until I can join Carol, but lately I've realized that I must let it go. And with the plunge of that last petal, I must also lay down my enduring reservations about whether I'd done enough. Otherwise, I'll risk shading the warm light that those seven years shined upon us.

The last words Carol spoke were with a nurse, who'd dropped in to ask how she was doing. Of course, the answer was, "I'm fine." Those two final and defining syllables contained the biggest lesson I learned from my wife. In living by those words, she embraced her circumstances as they were, and therefore understood humility at the deepest level. It took me the better part of my life to get there, but I am forever thankful that she let me catch up.

Will I still worry about it from time to time? With the way my mind works, yes. I'm not perfect, and never will be. But I'll always have the best seven years of my life, a gift of love and forgiveness that only Carol could have provided. It is a truth that will always outweigh my doubt.

I'd finished talking with Carol for the day, so I leaned in to kiss the white, engraved slab three times. "I love you, honey." I pressed my palm to her engraved name. "I'd stay longer, but I have to go to a meeting." I straightened up. "As of today, I'm officially on the Board of Directors for the cemetery. We have a lot of work to do to keep it looking nice up here."

I'll love you for the rest of my years.

On my way to the door, I scanned the room to see if anything needed to be fixed. Then, I turned back to my wife.

"That's all I'm saying."

the end

acknowledgements

In my lifetime, I never dreamed I would write a book. When Chad suggested that we write one together, I figured it would become what we discussed: lessons I learned in caring for Carol as it pertained to the medical system, insurance companies, caregiving, and therapists. When he returned the first chapter to me in his initial manuscript, I was floored. It wasn't a self-help caregiver's guide; it was a love story honoring the legacy of his mother and how she approached life, and ultimately, death. Chad, I can't thank you enough for what you have given me.

To my daughter-in-law Catherine, my gratitude for being an active participant in Carol's life, all your patience in the times I took Chad away from you to write the book, your professional insight as an author, and for lending your fantastic writing skills to the project.

Thank you to both Sean and Matthew for being the wonderful sons that you are. You supported me and my approach to caring for your mother and always were caring and respectful. You helped in so many ways, but none more than always being there in times when I just needed confirmation that I was not alone. Though you were states away, all your phone calls to check in on us, and your flowers for your mom on all occasions were little things that made a big difference. She felt your love.

Kyle Fager was an invaluable editor and friend from the very beginning. Your professional approach and calm demeanor gave secure and steady passage in developing this story. Also, your knowledge producing the physical book has kept us focused on the final product. Chad and I have been very fortunate to have your expertise available to us throughout.

Thank you to Lori Mross, Judith Thomas, and Mary Jane Platt for reading the early drafts and providing helpful insights and suggestions. You confirmed early on that this is a story worthy of a book.

My friend Dennis Ciccone provided helpful knowledge and insight into the world of publishing. It all seemed very daunting, but you provided guidance and counseling through all your experience in the business. You helped us understand the process in an unfamiliar world.

The photos of Carol and me on the front cover, back cover, and the start of chapter twelve were provided by Pam Ingram of Ingram Portrait Design, Sewickley, PA. You are a wonderful and kind person, Pam, as well as a great photographer.

Thank you, Mandy Stoffel, for your professional approach to the excellent design work for the book. When we started, I wanted a picture of Carol and me on the cover, and through your artistry, I was moved to something deeper. Kyle knew that I would like your work, and he was right.

Thank you to all my friends and family for the kind words of support. Your expressions of love and encouragement that I was doing enough for Carol provided me strength to continue the journey. Every little nod of recognition and pat on the back inspired me. My good friend Roger Entress said to me one day, "Take good care of yourself. You are the only one like you in Carol's life." How profound.

Thank you to Carol's cousin Jodi Jaynes and her husband David, who drove from Columbus, Ohio to be there for our family with each serious episode. They are living proof that just extending love and kindness makes a big difference to the worried patient and caregivers.

On my daily walk, I encountered Jodi Renner, who helped me talk through my disappointment that God wasn't present in my life to help ease my burden. Jodi explained that I was looking in the wrong place. As she said, I shouldn't be looking for God to help me, but rather, I should understand that God was present in me so that I could help Carol. Simple but enlightening.

Thank you also to my friend Tex Enoch, who visited with us at our home and said upon leaving, "Carol is the little engine that could." Those words spoke volumes.

My cancer is present but very much under control thanks to the good care of Dr. Shifeng Mao and his team at Allegheny General Hospital. He is a warm and caring doctor that takes his responsibilities personally.

And, finally, I have a chance to say I'm sorry to Doc Bartruff. Rest in Peace, Doc. You were a good man.

please visit

BESTSEVENYEARS.COM

for more information about
speaking engagements, book signings,
and to get in touch with the authors.

CPSIA information can be obtained
at www.ICGtesting.com
Printed in the USA
BVHW070537271118
534063BV00002B/58/P

9 781732 645530